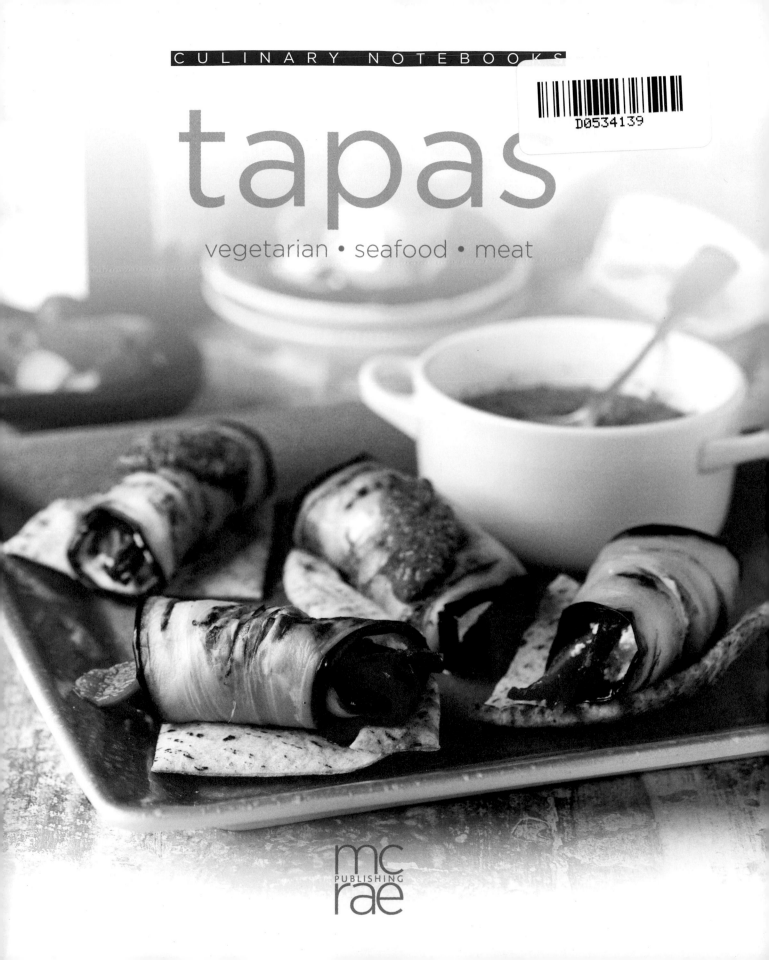

tapas

vegetarian • seafood • meat

mc
rae
PUBLISHING

This book was conceived,
edited and designed by
McRae Publishing Ltd
London

Copyright © 2012 McRae Publishing Ltd

All rights reserved. Unauthorized reproduction,
in any manner, is prohibited.

www.mcraepublishing.co.uk

Culinary Notebooks series

Project Director Anne McRae
Art Director Marco Nardi

TAPAS
Photography Brent Parker Jones
Text Carla Bardi
Editing Christine Price, Daphne Trotter
Food Styling Lee Blaylock
Food Styling Assistant Rochelle Seator
Prop Styling Lee Blaylock
Layouts Aurora Granata
Prepress Filippo Delle Monache

ISBN 978-88-6098-332-9

Printed in China

contents

getting started

There are 100 tempting tapas recipes in this book. Most are simple and quick to prepare. They are all rated for difficulty: 1 (simple), 2 (fairly simple), or 3 (challenging). The yields for each recipe have been calculated as starters (tapas). If serving the dishes as a main course, you will need to double the quantities. In these two pages we have highlighted 25 of the most enticing recipes, just to get you started!

● SIMPLE

BLACK OLIVE & ANCHOVY tapenade

FRIED ALMONDS
with thyme

BREAD, ANCHOVY
& CAPERBERRY salad

FRIED anchovies

BBQ MINI pork ribs

ORANGE SALAD with
dried fruit, nuts & olives

PISTO

TUNA & AVOCADO
salad

FAVA BEAN salad

● HEALTHY

SCALLOPS with bell peppers & onions

CLASSICS

GARLIC mushrooms **40**

PATATAS bravas **41**

TOMATO & ANCHOVY bread **45**

GARLIC SHRIMP **57**
with sherry

MIGAS **102**
de Almería

ONIONS **33**
with honey

SHRIMP fritters **78**

EDITOR'S CHOICE

HAM & CHEESE **89**
bocadillos

MEATBALLS **110**
in tomato sauce

SPICY CHORIZO tortilla **96**

BEST VEGGIE TAPAS | BEST FRIED TAPAS | BEST SEAFOOD TAPAS | BEST MEAT TAPAS | BEST TAPAS SALAD

VEGETARIAN **26**
empanadas

POTATO & HAM **116**
croquettes

STUFFED TOMATOES **62**
with tuna

CHICKEN LIVER & SHERRY **92**
salad

ARTICHOKE **7**
& MANCHEGO salad

vegetarian tapas

ARTICHOKE & MANCHEGO salad

Serves 4-6 • Preparation 15 minutes • Difficulty 1

Salad

4   young artichokes
     Freshly squeezed juice
     of 1 lemon
1/4 cup fresh dill
3   ounces (90 g) Manchego
     cheese, in shavings

Orange Dressing

     Freshly squeezed juice
     of 1 orange
2   tablespoons extra-virgin olive
     oil
1   teaspoon sherry vinegar
     Salt and freshly ground black
     pepper

Salad

1. Clean the artichokes by trimming the stalk and cutting off the top third of the bulb. Remove the tough outer leaves by bending them down and snapping them off at the base. When the tender heart is exposed, cut in half and remove any fuzzy choke with a knife. Slice very thinly.

2. Put the artichokes in a bowl and drizzle with the lemon juice. This will stop them from turning black.

Orange Dressing

1. Whisk the orange juice, oil, sherry vinegar, salt, and pepper in a small bowl until smooth.

2. Drain the artichokes of excess lemon juice. Add the dill and toss to combine. Drizzle with the dressing and toss lightly. Top with the cheese and serve.

If you liked this recipe, you will love these as well.

**POTATO, APPLE
& WALNUT** salad

ORANGE salad

ARTICHOKES with ham

8

Almonds are used in many Spanish dishes, from tapas to desserts. This simple appetizer goes beautifully with a glass of wine and a slice of Manchego cheese.

FRIED ALMONDS with thyme

¹/₄	cup (60 ml) extra-virgin olive oil
2	cups (300 g) whole blanched almonds
2-3	tablespoons fresh thyme leaves
	Salt and freshly ground black pepper
	Slices of Manchego cheese, to serve

Serves 6-8 • Preparation 5 minutes • Cooking 5-8 minutes • Difficulty 1

1. Heat the oil in a large frying pan over medium heat. Add the almonds and cook, stirring occasionally, until lightly golden and fragrant, 5-8 minutes.

2. Stir in the thyme leaves. Remove from the heat. Season with salt and pepper.

3. Spread out on a rimmed baking sheet, and let cool a little before serving with the cheese.

If you liked this recipe, you will love these as well.

ORANGE SALAD with dried fruit, nuts & olives

SALTED almonds

MEATBALLS with almonds & peas

ORANGE SALAD with dried fruit, nuts & olives

4	medium oranges, peeled
1	small red onion, thinly sliced
⅓	cup (90 ml) extra-virgin olive oil
2	tablespoons raspberry vinegar
	Salt and freshly ground black pepper
4	tablespoons golden raisins (sultanas), soaked in hot water for 15 minutes, then drained
20	black olives, pitted
2	tablespoons sunflower seeds
2	tablespoons blanched almonds, coarsely chopped
	Fresh mint, to garnish

Serves 4–6 • Preparation 15 minutes + 30 minutes to soak & chill • Difficulty 1

1. Remove the white pith from the oranges and slice the fruit crosswise, catching any juice in a bowl. Arrange the fruit on a serving platter and sprinkle with the red onion.

2. Whisk the oil, vinegar, orange juice, salt, and pepper in a small bowl until smooth. Spoon over the oranges.

3. Sprinkle with the golden raisins, olives, sunflower seeds, and almonds. Garnish with the mint.

4. Chill for 15 minutes before serving.

POTATO, APPLE & WALNUT salad

4   medium potatoes, peeled
2   large green apples, peeled, cored, and diced
1/3 cup (90 ml) freshly squeezed lemon juice
6   scallions (spring onions), chopped
1/2 cup (90 g) golden raisins (sultanas)
2   stalks celery, sliced
20   walnuts, shelled
1   cup (250 ml) mayonnaise
2   tablespoons coarsely chopped fresh cilantro (coriander)

Serves 6-8 • Preparation 15 minutes • Cooking 15-20 minutes • Difficulty 1

1. Cook the potatoes in salted boiling water until tender, 15-20 minutes.

2. Drizzle the apples with the lemon juice to prevent discoloration and set aside.

3. Combine the scallions, golden raisins, celery, and potatoes in a salad bowl.

4. Add the diced apple, walnuts, and mayonnaise, mixing gently but thoroughly. Sprinkle with the cilantro and serve.

SALTED almonds

Serves 2–4 • Preparation 10 minutes • Cooking 15–20 minutes • Difficulty 1

1	cup (150 g) whole almonds, shelled but with their skins	1/2	teaspoon coarse sea salt
1	tablespoon egg white, lightly beaten		

1. Preheat the oven to 350°F (180°C/gas 4).

2. Spread the almonds out on a baking sheet. Roast until lightly browned, 10–15 minutes.

3. Mix the egg white and salt in a small bowl. Add the almonds, stirring gently to coat. Pour onto the baking sheet, shaking to separate the nuts.

4. Return to the oven for 5 minutes, until the almonds have dried. Let cool completely.

5. Store in an airtight container until ready to serve.

ORANGE salad

Serves 4 • Preparation 15 minutes • Difficulty 1

4	artichokes		cheese, flaked
	Freshly squeezed juice of 1 lemon	1	tablespoon finely chopped fresh parsley
2	oranges, peeled and divided into segments	1/3	cup (90 ml) extra-virgin olive oil
5	ounces (150 g) aged Manchego or Parmesan		Salt and freshly ground black pepper

1. Clean the artichokes by trimming the stalks and cutting off the top third of the leaves. Remove the tough outer leaves by pulling them down and snapping them off. Cut in half and use a sharp knife to remove any fuzzy choke. Cut into thin wedges.

2. Place in a large salad bowl and drizzle with half the lemon juice. This will stop them from turning brown.

3. Put the oranges, cheese, and parsley in a large salad bowl. Drain the artichokes and add to the bowl.

4. Drizzle with the oil and remaining lemon juice and season with salt and pepper. Toss gently and serve.

MARINATED eggplant

Serves 4 • Preparation 15 minutes + 5 hours to drain & chill Cooking 15–20 minutes • Difficulty 2

2	medium eggplant (aubergines), with skin, cut into 1/2-inch (1-cm) thick slices	1	tablespoon finely chopped fresh parsley
		1	cup (100 g) pitted black olives
1	tablespoon coarse sea salt	1/2	cup (120 ml) white wine vinegar
5	tablespoons (75 ml) extra-virgin olive oil	1/2	cup (120 ml) water
4	cloves garlic, sliced	1	teaspoon freshly ground black pepper
1	red bell pepper (capsicum), sliced	1	teaspoon cayenne pepper

1. Place a layer of eggplant in a colander and sprinkle with coarse sea salt. Repeat, sprinkling each layer with salt. Let drain for 1 hour. Shake the salt off.

2. Heat the oil in a large frying pan over medium heat. Fry the eggplant in batches until tender and lightly browned, about 5 minutes. Drain on paper towels.

3. Layer the eggplant, garlic, bell pepper, parsley, and olives in a shallow glass or ceramic dish.

4. Combine the vinegar, water, and both types of pepper in a small saucepan over medium heat. Bring to a boil. Pour over the eggplant in the dish. Let cool to room temperature. Cover the dish and chill for at least 4 hours before serving.

MARINATED bell peppers

Serves 4–6 • Preparation 30 minutes + 2 hours to chill Cooking 10–15 minutes • Difficulty 2

4	red or yellow bell peppers (capsicums)	1/2	teaspoon untreated lemon zest
1	tablespoon capers, soaked in salted water before use	2	tablespoons balsamic vinegar
1	clove garlic, finely chopped	1/2	teaspoon smoked sweet paprika
3	tablespoons (45 ml) extra-virgin olive oil		

1. Broil (grill) the bell peppers until the skins are blackened all over, 10–15 minutes. Wrap in a plastic bag for 15 minutes, then remove the skins and seeds. Slice into strips and place in a shallow dish.

2. Add the capers, garlic, oil, lemon zest, balsamic vinegar, and paprika and mix well.

3. Cover with plastic wrap (cling film) and chill for at least 2 hours or overnight. This will allow the flavors to infuse. Serve warm or at room temperature.

SPINACH with garbanzo beans

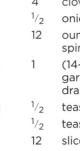
1 tablespoon extra-virgin olive oil + extra to drizzle
4 cloves garlic, finely chopped
$1/2$ onion, finely chopped
12 ounces (350 g) frozen spinach, thawed
1 (14-ounce/400-g) can garbanzo beans (chickpeas), drained
$1/2$ teaspoon ground cumin
$1/2$ teaspoon salt
12 slices bread, toasted

Serves 6 • Preparation 15 minutes • Cooking 10–15 minutes • Difficulty 1

1. Heat the oil in a large frying pan over medium heat. Add the garlic and onion and sauté until softened, 3–4 minutes. Stir in the spinach, garbanzo beans, cumin, and salt. Use the stirring spoon to lightly mash the beans as the mixture cooks. Simmer until heated through, 5–10 minutes.

2. Spread the spinach mixture on the toast and drizzle with a little extra oil. Serve warm.

FRESH GOAT CHEESE with cilantro sauce

1   cup (50 g) fresh cilantro
     (coriander) leaves
1/2 cup (25 g) fresh mint leaves
4   cloves garlic
1   green bell pepper (capsicum),
     seeded and chopped
2   jalapeno peppers, seeded
1   teaspoon hot paprika
1   teaspoon salt
1   cup (250 ml) extra-virgin olive
     oil
2   tablespoons sherry vinegar
8   ounces (250 g) fresh creamy
     goat cheese
     Freshly baked bread, cut in
     small pieces, to serve

Serves 6 • Preparation 15 minutes • Difficulty 1

1. Combine the cilantro, mint, garlic, bell pepper, jalapenos, paprika, salt, and half the oil in a food processor. Chop to a smooth paste. Add the remaining oil and sherry vinegar and process until smooth.

2. Put the cheese on a serving dish and spoon the sauce over the top. Serve with the bread.

With more than 300 million olive trees, Spain grows more olives than any other country in the world. Over 90 percent of the olives are made into oil, but the rest are destined for tables. Choose a mixture of green and black and large and small olives for this dish.

MARINATED olives

2	cups (200 g) mixed black and green Spanish olives
2	tablespoons extra-virgin olive oil
1	tablespoon freshly squeezed lemon juice
1	unwaxed orange, scrubbed but not peeled, cut into small chunks
2	sprigs fresh rosemary
1	fresh green chile, seeded and thinly sliced
1	small red bell pepper (capsicum), seeded and cut into small chunks
1	small yellow bell pepper (capsicum), seeded and cut into small chunks
20	cherry tomatoes, quartered

Serves 8 • Preparation: 15 minutes + 1–2 days to marinate • Difficulty 1

1. Put the olives in a large bowl and add the oil, lemon juice, chunks of orange, rosemary, and chile. Stir gently. Cover the bowl with plastic wrap (cling film) and place in the refrigerator.

2. Leave the olive mixture in the refrigerator for 1–2 days. Take it out a few times and give it a gentle stir. .

3. About an hour before serving, transfer the olives to a serving bowl, add the bell peppers and cherry tomatoes, and stir well. Let come to room temperature and serve.

If you liked this recipe, you will love these as well.

FRIED ALMONDS
with thyme

MARINATED
eggplant

MARINATED
bell peppers

STUFFED tomatoes

12   small tomatoes

6   hard-boiled eggs, cooled and peeled

$1/2$ cup (120 g) allioli (see page 82)

      Salt and freshly ground black pepper

2   tablespoons finely chopped fresh parsley + extra to garnish

Serves 6–12 • Preparation 30 minutes + 1 hour to chill • Difficulty 2

1. Peel the tomatoes, by cutting out the core with a sharp knife and making a "T"-shaped incision on the bottom of the tomato. Place in a pan of boiling water for 10 seconds, then plunge into a bowl of iced water. Remove the peel.

2. Slice the tops off the tomatoes, and just enough of their bases to remove the rounded ends so that they will sit squarely on a plate. Reserve the tops. Remove the seeds and insides using a teaspoon.

3. Mash the eggs with the allioli, salt, pepper, and parsley in a small bowl. Stuff the tomatoes with the mixture using a teaspoon, pressing the filling down to fill. Replace the lids on top. Chill for 1 hour. Sprinkle with parsley and serve.

BAKED TOMATOES andalusian style

6	large tomatoes, halved
2	cups (200 g) fresh bread crumbs
3	tablespoons finely chopped fresh parsley
	Salt and freshly ground black pepper
2	tablespoons butter
1	onion, chopped
I	tablespoon finely chopped fresh thyme
1¹/₂	cups (180 g) freshly grated Manchego cheese

Serves 6 • Preparation 15 minutes • Cooking 25–30 minutes • Difficulty 1

1. Preheat the oven to 350°F (180°C/gas 4).

2. Cut the tops off the tomatoes. Use a small teaspoon to remove the seeds and juice, setting aside in a bowl. Add the bread crumbs and parsley to the bowl. Season with salt and pepper.

3. Heat the butter in a medium frying pan. Add the onion and sauté until softened, 3–4 minutes. Add the bread crumb mixture and thyme and simmer for a few minutes. Stir in half the cheese then remove from the heat.

4. Stuff the mixture into the tomatoes. Top with the remaining cheese and bake for 20–25 minutes, until the tops are crisp and golden. Serve hot.

Tortillas are a classic Spanish dish. They are often served as tapas, but also make an excellent breakfast or light lunch or dinner. Don't confuse Spanish tortillas with the Mexican dish of the same name. In Spain, a tortilla is a type of potato omelet.

20

TORTILLA with arugula

¹/₄ cup (60 ml) extra-virgin olive oil + extra for the pan
1 pound (500 g) potatoes, peeled and sliced about ¹/₂ inch (1 cm) thick
1 large onion, thinly sliced
1 cup (250 ml) water
5 large eggs, lightly beaten
Salt and freshly ground black pepper
¹/₂ cup (60 g) freshly grated Manchego cheese
1 cup (50 g) arugula (rocket)

Serves 4–6 • Preparation 15 minutes • Cooking 20 minutes • Difficulty 1

1. Heat the oil in a medium, deep-sided, ovenproof frying pan over medium heat. Add the potatoes and onion. Stir gently until they start to sizzle and color a little, then pour in the water. Simmer gently until tender, about 10 minutes.

2. Pour off any excess liquid from the potatoes. Add the eggs to the pan, season with salt and pepper, and stir gently to mix. Sprinkle with the cheese. Simmer over medium heat until set on the bottom, about 5 minutes.

3. Preheat the broiler (grill) to high. Place the tortilla under the broiler until the cheese is bubbling and golden. Serve warm, topped with the arugula.

If you liked this recipe, you will love these as well.

POTATO & CHEESE
fritters

SPICY CHORIZO
tortilla

HAM & MANCHEGO
tortilla

GRILLED veggies

Serves 4–6 • Preparation 10 minutes • Cooking 25–35 minutes • Difficulty 1

4	medium zucchini (courgettes), thinly sliced lengthwise	1	large eggplant (aubergine) with skin, thinly sliced
1	red bell pepper (capsicum), seeded and cut in strips	8	tablespoons (120 ml) extra-virgin olive oil
1	yellow bell pepper (capsicum), seeded and cut in strips		Salt and freshly ground black pepper

1. Preheat a grill pan over high heat. Brush all the vegetables lightly with 2–3 tablespoons of oil.

2. Grill the zucchini until tender and marked with brown lines from the grill, 3–4 minutes each side. Place on a serving plate.

3. Grill the bell pepper strips and eggplant until tender and marked with brown lines from the grill, about 5 minutes each side. Add to the serving plate.

4. Season with salt and pepper. Drizzle with the remaining 5–6 tablespoons of oil and serve warm or at room temperature.

PAN-FRIED potatoes

Serves 6–8 • Preparation 15 minutes • Cooking 18–20 minutes • Difficulty 1

1½	pounds (750 g) whole small new potatoes	6	sun-dried tomatoes packed in oil, drained and finely chopped
½	cup (120 ml) extra-virgin olive oil	1	tablespoon brine-cured capers, drained
½	teaspoon sweet paprika	1	teaspoon dried oregano
	Salt		

1. Bring a large pot of salted water to a boil, add the potatoes, and cook until almost tender, about 10 minutes (depending on their size). Drain well and cut in half.

2. Heat the oil in a large frying pan over medium heat. Add the potatoes and sauté for 5 minutes.

3. Sprinkle with the paprika and season with salt. Add the sun-dried tomatoes and capers. Sauté until the potatoes are crisp, 3–5 minutes. Sprinkle with the oregano and sauté for 1 minute more. Serve hot.

EGGPLANT fritters

Serves 6-8 • Preparation 15 minutes • Cooking 20–30 minutes • Difficulty 2

2	eggplant (aubergines)	2	large eggs, lightly beaten
1	tablespoon finely chopped fresh parsley		Salt and freshly ground black pepper
10	leaves fresh basil, torn	1	cup (150 g) fine, dry bread crumbs
1	clove garlic, finely chopped	4	cups (1 liter) olive oil, for deep-frying
4	tablespoons freshly grated Parmesan cheese		

1. Preheat the oven to 400°F (200°C/gas 6).

2. Cut the eggplant in half and place on a baking sheet, cut-side up. Bake for 15–20 minutes, until tender and golden. Scoop out the flesh with a spoon, mashing it coarsely with a fork.

3. Mix the eggplant, parsley, basil, garlic, Parmesan, and eggs. Season with salt and pepper. Mix in enough bread crumbs to make a firm mixture. Shape into balls. Roll in the remaining bread crumbs.

4. Heat the oil in a deep-fryer or deep saucepan. Test the oil temperature by dropping in a small piece of bread. If it turns golden and bubbles to the surface, it is ready. Fry the fritters in batches until golden, about 5 minutes each batch. Remove with a slotted spoon and drain on paper towels. Serve hot.

BREAD FRITTERS with salsa

Serves 6-8 • Preparation 20 minutes • Cooking 20–30 minutes • Difficulty 2

Salsa		**Fritters**	
1	pound (500 g) tomatoes, chopped	8	cups (400 g) day-old bread, crumbled
1	red onion, chopped	4	large eggs, lightly beaten
2	chiles, finely chopped	½	cup (60 g) freshly grated Manchego cheese
2	tablespoons finely chopped fresh cilantro (coriander)	2	tablespoons finely chopped fresh parsley
2	tablespoons freshly squeezed lime juice		Salt and freshly ground black pepper
	Salt and freshly ground black pepper	4	cups (1 liter) olive oil, for deep-frying

Salsa

1. Combine the tomatoes, onion, chiles, cilantro, and lime juice in a bowl. Season with salt and pepper.

Fritters

1. Mix the bread, eggs, half the cheese, and parsley. Season with salt and pepper. Shape into fritters.

2. Heat the oil in a deep-fryer or deep saucepan. Fry the fritters in batches until golden, 4–5 minutes. Remove with a slotted spoon. Drain on paper towels.

3. Arrange on a heated serving dish. Sprinkle with the remaining cheese and serve hot with the salsa.

SPINACH with raisins & pine nuts

4 pounds (2 kg) fresh or frozen spinach
3 tablespoons (45 g) butter
3/4 cup (135 g) raisins
3/4 cup (135 g) pine nuts
   Salt

Serves 8–12 • Preparation 5 minutes • Cooking 10–15 minutes
Difficulty 1

1. Cook the spinach in a large pot of salted boiling water until just tender, 3–5 minutes. Drain well, squeezing out excess moisture.

2. Melt the butter in a large saucepan over medium heat. Sauté the raisins and pine nuts until lightly toasted, 3–5 minutes.

3. Add the spinach to the pan and cook for 5 minutes, stirring constantly, until the butter has all been absorbed. Season with salt. Serve hot.

STUFFED mushrooms

2 cups (120 g) day-old white bread, crusts removed

2 scallions (spring onions), white and pale green parts only, coarsely chopped

1 red bell pepper (capsicum), seeded and coarsely chopped

3¹/₂ ounces (100 g) fresh goat cheese

¹/₂ cup (25 g) finely chopped fresh cilantro (coriander)

¹/₂ cup (60 g) freshly grated aged Manchego or Parmesan cheese

¹/₂ teaspoon salt

¹/₄ teaspoon freshly ground black pepper

48 button mushrooms (about 1¹/₂ pounds/750 g), stems removed and caps cleaned

Serves 8-12 • Preparation 30 minutes • Cooking 15–20 minutes
Difficulty 1

1. Preheat the oven to 350°F (180°C/gas 4).

2. Pulse the bread in a food processor until finely chopped. Transfer to a bowl. Put the scallions, bell pepper, and goat cheese in the food processor and pulse until finely chopped. Transfer to the bowl with the bread. Stir in the cilantro, half the grated cheese, salt, and pepper.

3. Arrange the mushrooms, cup-side up, on a large baking sheet. Spoon a teaspoon of the stuffing mixture onto each cap. Sprinkle with the remaining cheese.

4. Bake until the mushrooms are tender and the filling is bubbling, 15–20 minutes. Serve hot.

Empanadas are a type of stuffed bread that can be baked or fried. They are popular in Spain and Portugal as tapas or snacks.

VEGETARIAN empanadas

Pastry

2	cups (300 g) all-purpose (plain) flour
$1/2$	teaspoon salt
$1/4$	cup (60 g) unsalted butter
2	tablespoons extra-virgin olive oil
1	large egg, beaten
$1/3$	cup (90 ml) ice water

Filling

3	tablespoons extra-virgin olive oil
1	onion, coarsely chopped
2	cloves garlic, finely chopped
1	red bell pepper (capsicum), coarsely chopped
$1/2$	green bell pepper (capsicum), coarsely chopped
2	tomatoes, coarsely chopped
	Salt and freshly ground black pepper
1	large egg, lightly beaten

Serves 6 • Preparation 30 minutes + 2 hours to chill • Cooking 35–40 minutes • Difficulty 2

Pastry

1. Combine the flour, salt, butter, oil, and egg in a food processor and pulse well. Slowly add the water until the dough starts to come together. Transfer to a lightly floured work surface and knead for 1 minute. Press into a ball, wrap in plastic wrap (cling film), and chill for 2 hours.

Filling

1. Preheat the oven to 375°F (190°C/gas 5). Oil a large baking sheet and place in the oven.

2. Heat the oil in a large frying pan over medium heat. Add the onion and garlic and sauté until softened, 3–4 minutes. Add the bell peppers and tomatoes and season with salt and pepper. Simmer until the vegetables are tender, about 15 minutes.

3. Transfer to a chopping board and coarsely chop with a knife.

4. Roll out the dough on a lightly floured work surface to about $1/8$ inch (3 mm) thick. Cut out six 6-inch (15-cm) circles. Place 1–2 tablespoons of filling on one-half of each circle, leaving a border free of filling around the edges. Spread the beaten egg around the borders and fold the pastry over the filling. Use a fork to press down on the edges to seal.

5. Transfer to the prepared baking sheet. Bake for 15–20 minutes, until golden brown. Serve hot or at room temperature.

STUFFED bell peppers

6 evenly-shaped, medium red bell peppers (capsicums)

3 tablespoons extra-virgin olive oil

1 small onion, finely chopped

8 ounces (250 g) ground (minced) pork

1 large tomato, peeled and coarsely chopped

1½ cups (300 g) short-grained Spanish rice, such as Bomba or Calasparra

1 tablespoon finely chopped fresh parsley

½ teaspoon saffron
Salt

Serves 6 • Preparation 30 minutes • Cooking 1 hour 40 minutes
Difficulty 2

1. Preheat the oven to 350°F (180°C/gas 4).

2. Cut off the stem ends of the bell peppers, keeping them to replace later as lids. Scrape out and discard the inner membranes with a teaspoon.

3. Heat the oil in a large frying pan over medium heat. Add the onion and sauté until softened, 3–4 minutes. Add the meat and brown lightly, 3–4 minutes. Add the tomato, rice, parsley, saffron, and salt.

4. Fill the bell peppers carefully and place standing upright in an ovenproof dish. Choose a baking dish that will hold the bell peppers snugly, fitting one against the other. Cover the dish with tin foil and bake for 1½ hours, until the bell peppers are softened. The rice will cook in the juices from the tomato and bell peppers. If it has not softened after about 1 hour, add a few tablespoons of water to the pan.

5. Serve warm or at room temperature.

GRILLED SWEET spanish peppers

2 cups (500 ml) extra-virgin olive oil

2 teaspoons sweet smoked paprika

1 clove garlic, thinly sliced

1 tablespoon black peppercorns

1 tablespoon fennel seeds

8 sweet red peppers (capsicums) (bell peppers or mild peppers)

8 sweet yellow peppers (capsicums) (bell peppers or mild peppers)

1¼ cups (300 ml) white wine vinegar

1¼ cups (300 ml) water

1 teaspoon salt

Serves 12–16 • Preparation 30 minutes + 10–15 minutes to rest • Cooking 20–25 minutes • Difficulty 2

1. Combine the oil, paprika, and garlic in a medium saucepan over low heat. Cook for 5 minutes, then let cool. Strain the oil through a fine-mesh sieve, discarding the garlic.

2. Dry-fry the peppercorns and fennel seeds in a small frying pan over medium heat until they release their aromas, about 1 minute. Add to the paprika oil and set aside.

3. Heat an overhead broiler (grill) to high. Spread the bell peppers out on two large baking sheets. Broil, turning often, for 10–15 minutes, until the skins are blackened. Put the hot bell peppers in plastic food bags, seal, and let cool for 15 minutes. When cool, pick off the skins, remove the stalks, scrape away the seeds, and slice into large pieces.

4. Bring the vinegar, water, and salt to a boil in a large saucepan. Add the peppers and simmer for 3 minutes. Drain well and add to the spiced oil.

5. Serve the bell peppers in the oil. This recipe makes a large quantity. Pack any leftovers in sterilized jars, fill with the oil, and seal for later use.

This is another classic tapa, originally from the Murcia region. There are many variations. In some areas, 2–3 lightly beaten eggs are stirred into the pan when the vegetables are almost cooked.

30

PISTO

¼ cup (60 ml) extra-virgin olive oil

2 medium potatoes, peeled and cut into ½-inch (1-cm) cubes

1 large onion, finely chopped

1 red bell pepper (capsicum), seeded and cut into small pieces

1 green bell pepper (capsicum), seeded and cut into small pieces

1 eggplant (aubergine), cut into small cubes

1 large zucchini (courgette), cut into small cubes

4 large tomatoes, coarsely chopped

Salt and freshly ground black pepper

¼ cup (60 ml) water, if needed

Serves 4-6 • Preparation 10 minutes • Cooking 35-40 minutes
Difficulty 1

1. Heat the oil in a large frying pan over medium heat. Add the potatoes and sauté for 8–10 minutes, until lightly browned.

2. Add the onion and bell peppers and cook, stirring often, until the onion is lightly browned, 8–10 minutes.

3. Add the eggplant and zucchini and cook, stirring often, for 5 minutes.

4. Stir in the tomatoes. Season with salt and pepper. Cook, adding the water if needed, for 10–15 minutes more, until the vegetables are tender.

5. Serve warm or at room temperature.

If you liked this recipe, you will love these as well.

MARINATED
eggplant

GRILLED VEGETABLE
salad

EGGPLANT ROLLS
with cilantro sauce

GRILLED VEGETABLE salad

2 large firm tomatoes, sliced

2 red bell peppers (capsicums), seeded and cut into large strips

1 green bell pepper (capsicum), seeded and cut into large strips

2 eggplant (aubergines), with skin, thickly sliced

1 large onion, quartered and divided into layers

6 tablespoons (90 ml) extra-virgin olive oil

2 cloves garlic, thinly sliced

2 tablespoons red wine vinegar

Salt and freshly ground black pepper

Serves 6–8 • Preparation 15 minutes • Cooking 20–25 minutes
Difficulty 1

1. Preheat a grill pan or barbecue to medium-high heat. Brush the tomatoes, bell peppers, eggplant, and onion with 2 tablespoons of the oil.

2. Grill all the vegetables a few at a time, turning frequently, until tender and cooked through, 20–25 minutes.

3. Place all the cooked vegetables in a shallow serving bowl. Add the garlic, and drizzle with the remaining oil and the vinegar. Season with salt and pepper. Mix gently and serve.

ONIONS with honey

20   small white onions, peeled and trimmed
3   tablespoons (45 ml) extra-virgin olive oil
3   tablespoons (45 ml) honey
1   teaspoon cumin seeds, crushed
     Salt and freshly ground black pepper

Serves 4-6 • Preparation 15 minutes • Cooking 20–30 minutes
Difficulty 1

1. Bring a large pan of lightly salted water to a boil. Add the onions and simmer until just tender, 15–20 minutes. Drain well, reserving 2 tablespoons of the cooking water.

2. Put the onions and reserved cooking water in a large frying pan with the oil, honey, and cumin. Season with salt and pepper. Cook, stirring often, over medium-high heat for 5–10 minutes, until the liquid is all absorbed and the onions are tender and golden.

3. Serve warm or at room temperature.

This spicy red sauce, called *mojo picón* in Spanish, is a classic originally from the Canary Islands. The sun-dried sweet peppers can be bell peppers or any other mild, sweet pepper. Buy them in Mediterranean foodstores or from online suppliers.

POTATOES with spicy red sauce

Potatoes

2 pounds (1 kg) small potatoes, with peel

Spicy Red Sauce

4 sun-dried sweet peppers (capsicums)

1/2 cup (120 ml) red wine vinegar

2 slices day-old white bread, crusts removed

6 cloves garlic, peeled

2 teaspoons red pepper flakes

1/2 teaspoon ground cumin

1/2 teaspoon salt

3/4 cup (180 ml) extra-virgin olive oil

Serves 6–8 • Preparation 15 minutes + 10 minutes to soak • Cooking 15–20 minutes • Difficulty 1

Potatoes

1. Cook the potatoes in a large pot of salted water until tender, 15–20 minutes. Drain, then return to the hot pan and let dry.

Spicy Red Sauce

1. Soak the sun-dried sweet peppers in the vinegar in a bowl until softened, about 10 minutes. Drain, reserving the vinegar.

2. Process the sweet peppers, bread, garlic, red pepper flakes, cumin, and salt in a food processor until coarsely chopped. With the machine running, gradually add the oil. Stir in a little of the reserved vinegar, according to taste.

3. Serve the sauce spooned over the potatoes.

If you liked this recipe, you will love these as well.

GRILLED SWEET
spanish peppers

PATATAS bravas

CRISP CALAMARI
with spicy red sauce

CRUMBED eggplant

Serves 4–6 • Preparation 10 minutes + 30 minutes to drain • Cooking 10–20 minutes • Difficulty 2

2	eggplant (aubergine), cut into ½-inch (1-cm) thick slices	1	cup (150 g) fine, dry bread crumbs
1	tablespoon coarse sea salt	⅓	cup (50 g) all-purpose (plain) flour
1	large egg	4	cups (1 liter) olive oil, for deep-frying
½	cup (120 ml) milk		Coarsely chopped fresh parsley, to garnish
2	cloves garlic, minced		

1. Place the eggplant in a colander and sprinkle with coarse sea salt. Let drain for 30 minutes. Shake off the excess salt. Pat dry with paper towels.

2. Beat the egg and milk in a small bowl until combined. Mix the garlic and bread crumbs in a separate dish. Put the flour in a third dish.

3. Dip the eggplant in the flour, then in the egg mixture, followed by the crumb mixture until well coated. Heat the oil in a deep-fryer or deep frying pan over medium-high heat.

4. Fry the eggplant in 2–3 batches until golden brown, 5–7 minutes. Remove with a slotted spoon and drain on paper towels. Serve hot garnished with parsley.

ZUCCHINI & CHEESE fritters

Serves 4–6 • Preparation 30 minutes + 20 minutes to chill Cooking 45 minutes • Difficulty 2

1	cup (200 g) long-grain rice		or other fresh soft goat cheese
1	large onion, chopped	2	large eggs
3	tablespoons finely chopped fresh parsley	2	tablespoons all-purpose (plain) flour
2	large zucchini (courgettes), grated		Salt and freshly ground black pepper
1½	ounces (45 g) Fontina cheese, grated	2	tablespoons extra-virgin olive oil
3	ounces (90 g) chèvre		

1. Put the rice and 2 cups (500 ml) of water in a saucepan and bring to a boil. Reduce the heat to low, cover, and simmer until tender, about 15 minutes. Remove from the heat and let stand, covered, for 5 more minutes.

2. Combine the cooked rice, onion, parsley, zucchini, Fontina, goat cheese, eggs, flour, and seasoning and stir to combine. Refrigerate for 20 minutes.

3. Heat the oil in a large, heavy frying pan. Add tablespoons of the mixture and fry until golden, 3–4 minutes each side. Drain on paper towels. Serve hot.

POTATO & CHEESE fritters

Serves 4–6 • Preparation 30 minutes + 1–2 hours to chill • Cooking: 10–15 minutes • Difficulty 1

1½	cups (375 g) cooked, mashed potato	1	tablespoon freshly squeezed lemon juice
1	cup (120 g) coarsely grated Manchego cheese		Finely grated zest of ½ untreated lemon
1	large egg, beaten		Freshly ground black pepper
3	scallions (spring onions), finely chopped	½	cup (75 g) all-purpose (plain) flour
3	tablespoons finely chopped fresh dill + extra to garnish	½	cup (120 ml) extra-virgin olive oil

1. Mix the mashed potato, cheese, egg, scallions, dill, and lemon juice and zest in a medium bowl until well combined. Season with pepper. Cover with plastic wrap (cling film) and chill until firm, 1–2 hours.

2. Using your hands, roll the mixture into balls the size of golf balls, then flatten slightly. Dip in the flour until well coated, shaking off the excess.

3. Heat the oil in a large, deep frying pan. Fry the fritters in batches until lightly browned on both sides, 5–7 minutes. Remove with a slotted spoon and drain on paper towels. Serve hot garnished with dill.

ASPARAGUS with mint dip

Serves 4–6 • Preparation 20 minutes • Cooking 15 minutes Difficulty 2

1	pound (500 g) asparagus, trimmed		bread crumbs
2	large eggs	½	cup (120 ml) plain yogurt
3	tablespoons freshly grated Parmesan	½	cup (120 ml) mayonnaise
4	cups (1 liter) olive oil, for frying	1	tablespoon finely chopped fresh mint
1	cup (150 g) fine, dry		Salt

1. Cook the asparagus in a pot of salted boiling water until almost tender, about 5 minutes. Drain well and dry carefully on a clean towel.

2. Beat the eggs and cheese in a small bowl. Heat the oil in a deep-fryer or deep saucepan. Test the oil temperature by dropping in a small piece of bread. If it immediately bubbles to the surface and begins to turn golden, the oil is ready.

3. Dip the asparagus in the eggs and then in the bread crumbs, making sure they are well coated. Fry the asparagus in small batches until golden brown, 4–5 minutes each batch. Drain on paper towels.

4. Beat the yogurt, mayonnaise, and mint in a small bowl. Season the asparagus with salt. Serve hot, with the mint dip on the side.

The cilantro sauce, or *mojo de cilantro*, in this recipe is another classic from the Canary Islands. It goes beautifully with these eggplant rolls but can also be served on potatoes instead of (or together with) the spicy red sauce on page 34. It is also delicious spooned over grilled or baked fish.

EGGPLANT ROLLS with cilantro sauce

Eggplant Rolls

2–3	eggplant (aubergines), with skin, thinly sliced lengthwise, to get 12 large slices
4	tablespoons (60 ml) extra-virgin olive oil
2	cloves garlic, sliced
1	cup (250 g) fresh cheese, such as ricotta
1/2	cup sun-dried tomato strips in oil, drained and chopped
2	roasted red bell peppers (capsicums), from a jar, drained and cut in strips
3	whole-wheat (wholemeal) pita breads, quartered and warmed, to serve

Cilantro Sauce

1	large bunch fresh cilantro (coriander)
4	cloves garlic, peeled
1/4	teaspoon ground cumin
1/2	teaspoon salt
3/4	cup (180 ml) extra-virgin olive oil
4–5	tablespoons (60–75 ml) water
1–2	teaspoons Spanish sherry vinegar

Serves 6–12 • Preparation 15 minutes + 10 minutes to soak • Cooking 15–20 minutes • Difficulty 2

Eggplant Rolls

1. Heat a grill pan over medium heat. Brush the eggplant with 2 tablespoons of oil and grill on both sides until softened. Let cool.

2. Heat the remaining oil in a small frying pan over medium heat. Add the garlic and sauté until softened, 1–2 minutes. Let cool for 10 minutes then stir into the ricotta cheese.

Cilantro Sauce

1. Process the cilantro, garlic, cumin, and salt in a food processor until smooth. With the machine running, gradually add the oil and enough water to make a smooth sauce. Stir in the vinegar, according to taste.

2. Spread some of the cheese filling over a slice of eggplant, sprinkle with sun-dried tomato, and top with a piece of roasted red pepper. Roll up the eggplant and set, seam-side down, on a plate. Repeat with all the eggplant and filling.

3. Put an eggplant roll on each piece of bread. Spoon a little cilantro sauce over the top and serve.

GARLIC mushrooms

¼   cup (60 ml) extra-virgin olive oil
12 ounces (350 g) button mushrooms, quartered
8   cloves garlic, finely chopped
3   tablespoons dry sherry
2   tablespoons freshly squeezed lemon juice
½   teaspoon red pepper flakes
¼   teaspoon smoked paprika
    Salt and freshly ground black pepper
2   tablespoons finely chopped fresh parsley
    Freshly baked bread, to serve

Serves 4–6 • Preparation 15 minutes • Cooking 8–10 minutes
Difficulty 1

1. Heat the oil in a large frying pan over medium heat. Add the mushrooms and sauté until just softened, 2–3 minutes.

2. Add the garlic, sherry, lemon juice, red pepper flakes, paprika, salt, and pepper. Simmer until the garlic and mushrooms are tender, about 5 minutes.

3. Sprinkle with the parsley and serve hot with the bread.

PATATAS bravas

1 cup (250 ml) extra-virgin olive oil
2 tablespoons finely chopped onion
2 cloves garlic, finely chopped
1½ tablespoons hot paprika
¼ teaspoon Tabasco sauce
¼ teaspoon ground thyme
½ cup (120 ml) ketchup
½ cup (120 ml) mayonnaise
Salt and freshly ground black pepper
2 pounds (1 kg) potatoes, peeled, and cut into 1-inch (2.5-cm) cubes
1 tablespoon finely chopped fresh parsley

Serves 6-8 • Preparation 15 minutes • Cooking 20 minutes • Difficulty 2

1. Heat 3 tablespoons of oil in a frying pan over medium heat. Add the onion and garlic and sauté until softened, 3–4 minutes. Turn off the heat and stir in the paprika, Tabasco sauce, and thyme. Transfer to a bowl and add the ketchup and mayonnaise. Season with salt and pepper. Set aside.

2. Lightly season the potatoes with salt and pepper. Heat the remaining oil in a large frying pan over medium-high heat. Fry the potatoes in 2–3 batches until crisp and golden brown. Drain on paper towels.

3. Mix the potatoes with the sauce just before serving. Garnish with the parsley and serve hot.

seafood tapas

SCALLOPS with bell peppers & onions

1/3 cup (90 ml) extra-virgin olive oil

1 (2-ounce/60-g) can anchovy fillets, drained

1 pound (500 g) large sea scallops

1 large red bell pepper (capsicum), seeded and coarsely chopped

1 large orange or yellow bell pepper (capsicum), seeded and coarsely chopped

1 red onion, coarsely chopped

2 cloves garlic, thinly sliced

1 1/2 teaspoons finely grated untreated lemon zest

1 teaspoon finely grated unwaxed lime zest

Freshly ground black pepper

Fresh parsley leaves, to garnish

Serves 6–8 • Preparation 15 minutes • Cooking 15 minutes • Difficulty 1

1. Heat the oil and anchovies in a large frying pan over medium-high heat, stirring constantly until the anchovies dissolve into the oil. Add the scallops, and cook until just browned on both sides, 3–4 minutes. Remove from the pan with a slotted spoon and set aside.

2. Combine the bell peppers, onion, garlic, and lemon and lime zest in the pan with the anchovy-flavored oil. Season with pepper and sauté until the onion and bell peppers have just softened, about 10 minutes.

3. Return the scallops to the pan and reheat. Serve hot, garnished with the parsley.

If you liked this recipe, you will love these as well.

GRILLED SEAFOOD
salad

VANILLA SCALLOPS
with roasted tomato salsa

BAKED scallops

BLACK OLIVE & ANCHOVY tapenade

1   baguette (French loaf), sliced

4   cups (400 g) whole, pitted black olives

1   (2-ounce/60-g) can anchovy fillets, drained

1   clove garlic, chopped

2   tablespoons brine-cured capers, drained + extra, to garnish

1   teaspoon fresh thyme

1   teaspoon fresh rosemary

3   tablespoons freshly squeezed lemon juice

¼   cup (60 ml) extra-virgin olive oil

Serves 6–8 • Preparation 15 minutes • Cooking 4–5 minutes • Difficulty 1

1. Preheat the oven to 400°F (200°C/gas 6). Spread the bread out on a baking sheet. Bake for 4–5 minutes, until crisp and golden brown. Set aside.

2. Combine the olives, anchovies, garlic, capers, thyme, rosemary and lemon juice in a food processor. Add the oil in a slow, steady trickle with the machine running, until a smooth paste is formed.

3. Spread the olive paste on the toast. Top each slice with 1–2 capers and serve.

TOMATO & ANCHOVY bread

1   baguette (French loaf), sliced
12   cherry tomatoes, coarsely
        chopped
1   (2-ounce/60-g) can anchovy
        fillets, drained
        Freshly ground black pepper
¼   cup (60 ml) extra-virgin olive
        oil

Serves 8–10 • Preparation 10 minutes • Difficulty 1

1. Place the bread on a large work surface or board. Top each slice with tomatoes and anchovies,

2. Season with the pepper, drizzle with the oil, and serve.

This salad is simple, elegant, and delicious, but it does depend on high-quality ingredients. Choose a firm bread that will not break up too easily, the tastiest cherry tomatoes, the freshest mint, and the very best olive oil you can afford.

BREAD, ANCHOVY & CAPERBERRY salad

4	thick slices firm-textured bread, torn or chopped into bite-size chunks
$1/4$	cup (60 ml) extra-virgin olive oil
2	tablespoons sherry vinegar
12	canned anchovy fillets, drained
	Freshly ground black pepper
16	green olives, pitted
12	cherry tomatoes, halved
12	caperberries
	Fresh mint leaves

Serves 4-6 • Preparation 10 minutes + 30 minutes to stand • Difficulty 1

1. Put the bread in a medium bowl. Add the oil, sherry vinegar, and anchovies and season generously with pepper. Toss gently then let stand at room temperature for 30 minutes.

2. Add the olives, cherry tomatoes, caperberries, and mint. Toss gently and serve.

If you liked this recipe, you will love these as well.

BLACK OLIVE & ANCHOVY tapenade

TOMATO & ANCHOVY bread

ROASTED TOMATO & SERRANO toasts

MARINATED baby octopus

Serves 6–8 • Preparation 10 minutes + 1 hour to marinate
Cooking 2–3 minutes • Difficulty 1

1/2	cup (120 ml) extra-virgin olive oil	2	teaspoons finely chopped fresh oregano
	Finely grated zest of 1 untreated lemon		Salt and freshly ground black pepper
2	tablespoons freshly squeezed lemon juice	1 1/2	pounds (750 g) baby octopus, cleaned
4	shallots, finely sliced		Salad greens, to serve

1. Mix the oil, lemon zest, lemon juice, shallots, and oregano in a large bowl. Season with salt and pepper. Add the octopus and toss gently in the marinade. Set aside to marinate for 1 hour.

2. Heat a grill pan over high heat, lightly brushing it with oil. Add the octopus, and cook—basting with the marinade—until tender, 2–3 minutes.

3. Serve hot or at room temperature with the salad.

GARLIC SHRIMP fritters

Serves 6 • Preparation 30 minutes + 20 minutes to marinate • Cooking 6–8 minutes • Difficulty 1

2	pounds (1 kg) shrimp (prawns), peeled and deveined		Freshly squeezed juice of 2 lemons
4	cloves garlic, finely chopped		Freshly ground black pepper
1	small red chile, seeded and finely chopped		Lime wedges, to garnish
1/4	cup (60 ml) extra-virgin olive oil		

1. Put the shrimp in a shallow dish. Combine the garlic, chile, oil, lemon juice, and pepper in a small bowl. Pour this mixture over the shrimp and let marinate for 20 minutes.

2. Heat the marinade in a large frying pan over medium-high heat. Cook the shrimp for 3–4 minutes on each side, depending on size, until pink and cooked through.

3. Place in individual serving dishes. Pour the juices from the pan over the top. Garnish with the lime and serve hot.

SQUID with garlic & capers

Serves 6 • Preparation: 15 minutes + 1 hour to chill
Cooking 12–15 minutes • Difficulty 2

Poaching Liquid

1	carrot, chopped		Juice of 2 lemons
1	onion, chopped	4	cloves garlic, finely chopped
4	cups (1 liter) water		Salt and freshly ground black pepper
	Juice 1 lemon	1	tablespoon fresh thyme
1/2	cup (50 g) capers		
4	squid tubes, about 6 ounces (180 g) each		**Salad**
		2	tomatoes, chopped
Marinade		2	teaspoons capers
3/4	cup (180 ml) extra-virgin olive oil	1	tablespoon finely chopped fresh parsley

Poaching Liquid

1. Combine the carrot, onion, water, lemon juice, and capers in a saucepan. Bring to a boil and simmer for 10 minutes. Add the squid and simmer until tender, 4–5 minutes.

Marinade

1. Combine the marinade ingredients in a bowl. Drain the squid and cut into 1/4-inch (5-mm) rings. Add to the marinade and chill for 1 hour.

Salad

1. Mix the tomatoes, capers, and parsley in a bowl. Add the squid to the salad. Use 1/4 cup (60 ml) of the marinade as a dressing and serve.

MARINATED sardines

Serves 6–8 • Preparation 20 minutes + 8 hours to gather flavor • Cooking 25 minutes • Difficulty 2

1 1/2	pounds (750 g) fresh sardines	1/2	cup (120 ml) water
2	onions, cut into thin rings	1/4	teaspoon ground cinnamon
1	carrot, thinly sliced lengthwise	1	bay leaf
		6	peppercorns
1	tablespoon finely chopped fresh parsley	1	tablespoon fresh thyme leaves
1/2	cup (120 ml) white wine vinegar	1/2	teaspoon salt
		2	tablespoons extra-virgin olive oil

1. Preheat the oven to 350°F (180°C/gas 4).

2. Cut the fins off the sardines and remove the backbones, leaving the heads and tails intact. Arrange the fish in a shallow baking dish and cover with the onions, carrot, and parsley.

3. Mix the vinegar, water, cinnamon, bay leaf, peppercorns, thyme, salt, and oil in a small bowl. Drizzle over the fish in the dish. Cover the dish with a lid or aluminum foil. Bake for 25 minutes.

4. Let cool completely at room temperature. Set aside for at least 8 hours before serving.

This is a regional dish from Murcia, a coastal region of southeastern Spain. As simple as it is delicious, be sure to serve this salad with lots of freshly baked bread to mop up the juices.

MURCIAN salad

Salad

2	large red bell peppers (capsicums)
2	tablespoons extra-virgin olive oil
4	ripe, round tomatoes, quartered
6	scallions (spring onions), trimmed
1	(8-ounce/250-g) can tuna, drained and crumbled with a fork
2	hard-boiled eggs, halved
12	large black olives
	Freshly baked, crusty bread

Dressing

$^1/_2$	cup (120 ml) extra-virgin olive oil
$^1/_4$	cup (60 ml) red wine vinegar
	Salt and freshly ground black pepper

Serves 4 • Preparation 15 minutes • Difficulty 1

Salad

1. Brush the bell peppers with the oil. Broil (grill) under a hot broiler, skin-side up, until the skin is blackened. Place in a plastic bag and let rest for 15 minutes. Remove the skin from the bell peppers and cut into long strips.

2. Arrange the tomatoes, scallions, and bell peppers on four salad plates. Top with the tuna, eggs, and olives.

Dressing

1. Whisk the oil and vinegar with a pinch of salt and pepper in a small bowl.

2. Drizzle the dressing over each salad and serve with plenty of bread to mop up the dressing and juices.

If you liked this recipe, you will love these as well.

BREAD, ANCHOVY & CAPERBERRY salad

SALT COD, ORANGE & OLIVE salad

FAVA BEAN salad

CALAMARI salad

Calamari
2	pounds (1 kg) calamari (squid), cleaned
1	onion, chopped
1	clove garlic, finely chopped
1	cup (250 ml) dry white wine
1/2	cup (120 ml) water

Dressing
2	tablespoons finely chopped shallots
2	cloves garlic, finely chopped
1/2	cup (120 ml) extra-virgin olive oil
2	teaspoons finely grated untreated lemon zest
1/2	cup (120 ml) freshly squeezed lemon juice
	Salt and freshly ground black pepper

Serves 8-10 • Preparation 30 minutes + 15 minutes to rest • Cooking 1 hour • Difficulty 2

Calamari

1. Slice the calamari bodies into rings. Cut the tentacles from the head, discarding the head.

2. Put the onion, garlic, wine, and water in a saucepan and bring to a boil. Add the calamari. Turn the heat down to low, cover, and simmer for 1 hour.

Dressing

1. Whisk the shallots, garlic, oil, lemon zest, lemon juice, salt, and pepper in a small bowl.

2. Drain the calamari and let cool a little. Toss with the dressing. Cover and let rest for 15 minutes before serving.

GRILLED OCTOPUS with bell peppers

2   red bell peppers (capsicums), seeded and cut into strips

1/2   cup (120 g) sun-dried tomatoes, drained and finely chopped

Freshly squeezed juice of 1 lime

Freshly squeezed juice of 1 lemon

2   tablespoons finely chopped thyme

1/2   cup (120 ml) extra-virgin olive oil + extra to drizzle

2   pounds (1 kg) octopus, cleaned and cut in small pieces

1   bunch arugula (rocket)

Salt and freshly ground black pepper

Lime or lemon wedges, to garnish

Serves 8 • Preparation 20 minutes + 15 minutes to rest • Cooking 15–20 minutes • Difficulty 2

1. Preheat the oven to 450°F (230°C/gas 8). Arrange the bell peppers on a baking sheet and roast for 10–12 minutes, until the skin is charred. Enclose in a plastic bag and set aside for 15 minutes.

2. Preheat a grill pan or barbecue to very hot. Combine the sun-dried tomatoes, lime juice, lemon juice, thyme, and oil in a large bowl. Add the octopus and stir gently. Let marinate at room temperature for 10–15 minutes.

3. When the bell peppers are cool, remove the skins with fingertips. Slice the flesh into wide strips.

4. Grill the octopus in the grill pan or barbecue until tender, 5–6 minutes. Spoon the marinade over as you cook.

5. Arrange the arugula, bell peppers, and octopus in six to eight serving plates. Drizzle with extra oil, season with salt and pepper, garnish with lime or lemon wedges, and serve.

For the best results with this salad, use very fresh seafood. The trick to buying fresh seafood is to see if it passes the "sniff test." Very fresh seafood has almost no odor, so hold it to your nose and sniff deeply before buying.

54

GRILLED SEAFOOD salad

Dressing
$1/2$	cup (120 ml) extra-virgin olive oil
3	tablespoons freshly squeezed lemon juice
2	tablespoons finely chopped fresh parsley
	Salt and freshly ground black pepper

Salad
1	pound (500 g) calamari, bodies and tentacles, cleaned
1	pound (500 g) small shrimp (prawns), peeled and deveined
8	ounces (250 g) small bay scallops
1	small head radicchio, shredded
1	cup (50 g) arugula (rocket) leaves
	Salt and freshly ground black pepper

Serves 6–8 • Preparation 30 minutes • Cooking 10–15 minutes
Difficulty 2

Dressing

1. Whisk the oil, lemon juice, parsley, salt, and pepper in a small bowl.

Salad

1. Heat a grill pan or barbecue over medium-high heat. Place the calamari, shrimp, and scallops in a medium bowl. Add 2 tablespoons of the dressing and toss to coat. Grill the seafood in batches until browned and cooked through, about 2 minutes on each side for the shrimp and calamari, and 1 minute each side for the scallops.

2. Slice the grilled calamari bodies and place in a clean bowl with all the grilled seafood.

3. Add the radicchio and arugula and toss with the remaining dressing. Serve at room temperature.

If you liked this recipe, you will love these as well.

GRILLED OCTOPUS
with bell peppers

SHRIMP & CHORIZO
skewers

CRISP CALAMARI
with spicy red sauce

SPICY garlic shrimp

1/4   cup (60 ml) extra-virgin olive oil

4   cloves garlic, finely chopped

1   teaspoon red pepper flakes

1   pound (500 g) shrimp (prawns)

1   teaspoon sweet paprika

   Freshly squeezed juice of 1 lemon

1/3   cup (90 ml) dry sherry

   Salt and freshly ground black pepper

1   tablespoon finely chopped fresh parsely

   Freshly baked bread, to serve

Serves 4-6 • Preparation 15 minutes • Cooking 5–10 minutes
Difficulty 1

1. Heat the oil in a large saucepan over medium heat. Add the garlic and red pepper flakes and sauté until the garlic is softened, 3-4 minutes.

2. Increase the heat to high and add the shrimp, paprika, lemon juice, and sherry. Sauté until the shrimp turns pink, 2–3 minutes.

3. Season with salt and pepper and sprinkle with the parsley. Serve hot, with plenty of fresh bread.

GARLIC SHRIMP with sherry

5 tablespoons (75 ml) extra-virgin olive oil
4 cloves garlic, thinly sliced
1 pound (500 g) large shrimp (prawns), peeled and deveined
3 tablespoons (45 ml) medium sherry
  Salt and freshly ground black pepper
2 tablespoons coarsely chopped fresh parsley

Serves 4-6 • Preparation 15 minutes • Cooking 6-8 minutes • Difficulty 1

1. Heat the oil in a large frying pan over medium-high heat. Add the garlic and sauté until just beginning to soften, 1-2 minutes. Add the shrimp and sauté until they start to turn pink, 2-3 minutes.

2. Pour in the sherry and simmer until the shrimp are cooked through, 1-2 minutes. Season with salt and pepper. Sprinkle with the parsley and serve hot.

Be sure to let the octopus cool in the cooking water. This makes the flesh very tender and succulent.

OCTOPUS galician style

1	medium octopus or several baby octopus, about 1 pound (500 g) total weight, cleaned
1	bay leaf
$^1/_2$	onion
$^1/_4$	cup (60 ml) white wine vinegar
4	potatoes, peeled and cut into bite-size chunks
2	tablespoons finely chopped fresh parsley
$^1/_3$	cup (90 ml) extra-virgin olive oil
1	teaspoon sweet paprika
$^1/_2$	teaspoon salt

Serves 4–6 • Preparation 15 minutes + 4 hours to stand • Cooking 1 hour • Difficulty 2

1. Put the octopus in a large saucepan. Add the bay leaf, onion, and vinegar, bring to a gentle boil, then simmer until tender, about 1 hour. Turn off the heat and let cool in the cooking water. Leave in the water for at least 4 hours.

2. Cook the potatoes in salted boiling water until tender, about 10 minutes. Drain well.

3. Slice the octopus into 1-inch (2.5-cm) chunks and place in a salad bowl. Add the potatoes and parsley. Drizzle with the oil and sprinkle with the paprika and salt. Toss gently and serve.

If you liked this recipe, you will love these as well.

MARINATED
baby octopus

GRILLED OCTOPUS
with bell peppers

OCTOPUS TERRINE
with potato salad

TUNA & AVOCADO salad

1   (12-ounce/350-g) can tuna in water, drained and flaked with a fork

2–3   tablespoons mayonnaise

3   scallions (spring onions), thinly sliced

1   red bell pepper (capsicum), seeded and finely chopped

2   cloves garlic, finely chopped

2   teaspoons balsamic vinegar

    Salt and freshly ground black pepper

2   small ripe avocados, halved and pitted

Serves 4 • Preparation 15 minutes • Difficulty 1

1. Combine the tuna, mayonnaise, scallions, bell pepper, garlic, and balsamic vinegar in a bowl. Season with salt and pepper and mix well.

2. Use a teaspoon to fill the avocado halves with the tuna mixture. Serve at room temperature.

SALT COD, ORANGE & OLIVE salad

14	ounces (400 g) salt cod
1	cup (250 ml) cold milk
4	large and juicy oranges, peeled and chopped
1	cup (100 g) black olives, pitted and halved
4	scallions (spring onions), chopped
1/4	cup (60 ml) extra-virgin olive oil
1	tablespoon white wine vinegar
3/4	cup (180 ml) water
	Salt
1	teaspoon sweet paprika
3	hard-boiled eggs, sliced or cut into wedges, to garnish

Serves 8 • Preparation 20 minutes + 26 hours to soak and chill
Cooking 20 minutes • Difficulty 2

1. Soak the salt cod in cold water for 24 hours, changing the water two or three times. Drain well.

2. Preheat the oven to 350°F (180°C/gas 4). Put the salt cod in a roasting pan and roast for 20 minutes, until golden brown. Pour the milk over the fish and set aside for at least one hour. Drain off the liquid, then flake the fish, removing any skin and bones.

3. Combine the fish, oranges, olives, and scallions in a serving bowl. Pour in the oil, vinegar, and water. Dust with the paprika and mix gently.

4. Cover the bowl and chill for at least one hour. Garnish with the eggs and serve.

If preferred, use 12 ounces (350 g) of fresh tuna to make this dish. Cook the tuna in a small frying pan over medium-low heat with a little oil until tender, 3–4 minutes. Break up with a fork and add to the recipe instead of the canned tuna.

STUFFED TOMATOES with tuna

2	cups (500 ml) fish stock
1	cup (200 g) short-grain rice
1	teaspoon sweet paprika
3	tablespoons extra-virgin olive oil
1	onion, finely chopped
2	cloves garlic, finely chopped
6	large tomatoes
1	(12-ounce/350-g) can tuna, drained
3	tablespoons finely chopped fresh parsley
1	tablespoon dry white wine
	Salt and freshly ground black pepper
6	tablespoons freshly grated Manchego cheese

Serves 6 • Preparation 20 minutes • Cooking 50 minutes • Difficulty 2

1. Bring the fish stock to a boil in a medium saucepan. Add the rice and paprika. Simmer until tender, about 15 minutes.

2. Preheat the oven to 375°F (190°C/gas 5). Heat the oil in a frying pan over medium-high heat. Add the onion and garlic and sauté until softened, 3–4 minutes.

3 . Cut the tops off the tomatoes and set aside. Use a teaspoon to scoop out the flesh. Reserve the tomato shells and finely chop the flesh. Add the flesh to the pan with onions, along with the parsley and wine. Simmer for about 5 minutes.

4. Add the rice and tuna and simmer for 2–3 minutes. Season with salt and pepper. Fill the tomatoes and sprinkle with the cheese. Cover with the reserved tops.

5. Bake the tomatoes for 20 minutes, until softened. Serve warm or at room temperature.

If you liked this recipe, you will love these as well.

STUFFED
tomatoes

BAKED TOMATOES
andalusian style

STUFFED
bell peppers

SARDINES in spicy marinade

24 large sardines (pilchards), ready to cook

2/3 cup (100 g) all-purpose (plain) flour

1/2 cup (120 ml) extra-virgin olive oil

6 cloves garlic, finely chopped

1 teaspoon red pepper flakes

1 tablespoon white wine vinegar

1 bay leaf

1 sprig rosemary

Salt and freshly ground black pepper

1 cup (250 ml) water

Serves 6–8 • Preparation 15 minutes + 1 hour to marinate • Cooking 20 minutes • Difficulty 1

1. Dredge the sardines in the flour, shaking off any excess. Heat the oil in a large frying pan over medium heat. Fry the sardines until golden brown, about 5 minutes on each side. Drain well on paper towels and place in a ceramic dish.

2. Add the garlic and red pepper flakes to the frying pan and sauté until softened, 3–4 minutes. Add the vinegar, bay leaf, and rosemary and simmer until the vinegar evaporates. Season with salt and pepper, add the water, and simmer for 5 minutes.

3. Pour the sauce over the sardines. Let marinate for at least 1 hour before serving.

SPICY clams

1¼ pounds (600 g) small clams, in shell
2 tablespoons extra-virgin olive oil
1 small onion, finely chopped
1 stalk celery, sliced
3 cloves garlic, finely chopped
2 teaspoons finely grated ginger
1 teaspoon red pepper flakes
1 teaspoon ground turmeric
2 tablespoons chopped fresh parsley + extra to serve
¼ cup (60 ml) dry white wine
Salt and freshly ground black pepper

Serves 4-6 • Preparation 20 minutes + 1 hour to soak • Cooking 10 minutes • Difficulty 1

1. Soak the clams in a large bowl of cold water for one hour

2. Heat the oil in a large frying pan over medium heat. Add the onion, celery, garlic, ginger, red pepper flakes, turmeric, and parsley and sauté until softened, about 5 minutes.

3. Add the clams and wine, cover, and simmer for about 5 minutes, shaking the pan occasionally, until all the clams are open. Discard any that have not opened. Season with salt and pepper.

4. Serve hot, garnished with the extra parsley.

This is an unusual recipe but you really should try it. The vanilla goes very well with the smooth rich flavor of the scallops.

VANILLA SCALLOPS with roasted tomato salsa

Roasted Tomato Salsa

12	tomatoes, halved
6	tablespoons (90 ml) extra-virgin olive oil
2	stalks celery, finely chopped
½	bulb fennel, blanched
	Freshly squeezed juice of ½ lime
1	garlic clove, crushed
2	tablespoons finely chopped fresh parsley

Scallops

½	cup (120 g) butter, softened
1	vanilla pod, seeds only
¼	cup (60 ml) extra-virgin olive oil
12	large scallops, corals removed
	Salt and freshly ground black pepper

Serves 4–6 • Preparation 20 minutes + 1 hour to soak • Cooking 20–25 minutes • Difficulty 2

Roasted Tomato Salsa

1. Preheat the oven to 400°F (200°C/gas 6). Put the tomatoes, cut-side up, on a baking sheet. Drizzle with 2 tablespoons of oil and season with salt. Roast until softened, 15–20 minutes. Cut into large pieces.

Scallops

1. Mix the butter and vanilla seeds in a small bowl.

2. Heat the oil in a large frying pan over medium-high heat. Add the scallops and sear for 30 seconds. Season with salt and pepper. Turn the scallops over, add the vanilla butter and cook until tender, about 1 more minute. Remove from the heat and keep warm.

3. Combine the roasted tomatoes, the remaining oil, celery, fennel, lime juice, garlic, and parsley in a food processor. Blend until coarsely chopped. Serve warm with the scallops.

If you liked this recipe, you will love these as well.

SCALLOPS with bell peppers & onions

GRILLED SEAFOOD salad

BAKED scallops

CLAMS with chorizo

2   pounds (1 kg) clams, in shell
1   pound (500 g) fresh chorizo, coarsely chopped
1   large onion, cut into thin wedges
1   (14-ounce/400-g) can chopped tomatoes
2   cups (500 ml) white wine
¼   cup (60 ml) extra-virgin olive oil

Serves 6–8 • Preparation 20 minutes + 1 hour to soak • Cooking 5–10 minutes • Difficulty 2

1. Soak the clams in a large bowl of cold water for 1 hour.

2. Place the clams in a large frying pan. Add the chorizo, onion, tomatoes, and wine. Cover and set over high heat. Steam until all the clams open up, 5–10 minutes, shaking the pan often. Discard any clams that do not open.

3. Drizzle the oil over the cooked clams. Spoon the clams into small serving bowls. Strain the cooking liquid through a fine-mesh sieve and drizzle over the bowls. Serve warm.

CLAMS with beans

2 pounds (1 kg) clams, in shell
2 tablespoons extra-virgin olive oil
1 garlic clove, finely chopped
1 onion, finely chopped
1 ripe tomato, chopped
1 bay leaf
1 cup (250 ml) white wine
1/2 cup (120 ml) water
1 (14 ounce/400-g) can cannellini beans, drained
Salt and freshly ground black pepper
2 tablespoons finely chopped fresh parsley

Serves 6–8 • Preparation 20 minutes + 1 hour to soak • Cooking 15–20 minutes • Difficulty 2

1. Soak the clams in a large bowl of cold water for 1 hour.

2. Heat the oil in a large frying pan over medium heat. Add the garlic and onion and sauté until softened, 3–4 minutes. Add the tomato and bay leaf and sauté for 2–3 minutes. Add the wine, water, and clams, cover, and simmer until all the clams open up, 5–10 minutes, shaking the pan often. Discard any clams that do not open.

3. Uncover the pan and add the beans. Season with salt and pepper and stir gently for 2–3 more minutes. Serve hot, garnished with the parsley.

This is a striking tapa that takes some time and skill to prepare, but is really worth the effort.

OCTOPUS TERRINE with potato salad

Terrine

5	pounds (2 kg) frozen octopus tentacles, thawed
1	teaspoon sweet paprika
½	cup (25 g) finely chopped fresh parsley

Potato Salad

2	pounds (1 kg) potatoes, peeled
½	cup (120 ml) extra-virgin olive oil
1	sweet red onion, finely diced
1	tablespoon smoked sweet paprika
	Salt

Serves 12 • Preparation 1 hour + 4 hours to cool • Cooking 50–70 minutes • Difficulty 3

Terrine

1. Cook the octopus in a large pan of water until tender, 30–40 minutes. Leave in the water until cool, at least 4 hours.

2. Line a round or rectangular 12-inch (30-cm) long terrine mold with plastic wrap (cling film). Trim the tentacles to the same length as the terrine mold. Place in a bowl, add the paprika and half the parsley. Arrange the tentacles in the terrine mold, using smaller tentacles to fill any gaps. Cover with plastic wrap, close, and chill overnight.

Potato Salad

1. Cook the potatoes in a large saucepan of salted water until tender 20–30 minutes. Drain and let cool. Place in a large bowl and crush with a fork until coarsely mashed. Add the oil, onion and paprika. Season with salt and mix well.

2. Slice the octopus terrine. Serve with the potato salad at room temperature.

If you liked this recipe, you will love these as well.

MARINATED
baby octopus

GRILLED OCTOPUS
with bell peppers

OCTOPUS
galician style

SHRIMP & CHORIZO skewers

2 tablespoons extra-virgin olive oil

2 shallots, finely sliced

1 pound (500 g) chorizo, cut in thick slices

2 cups (500 ml) red wine

2 bay leaves

4 sprigs thyme

2 teaspoons chile oil

16 large shrimp (prawns), peeled and deveined

2 tablespoons finely chopped fresh parsley

Serves 4 • Preparation 20 minutes • Cooking 10–15 minutes
Difficulty 1

1. Heat the oil in a saucepan over medium heat. Add the shallots and sauté until softened, 3–4 minutes. Remove the shallots and set aside.

2. Add the chorizo to the same pan and sauté for 2–3 minutes. Add the wine, bay leaves, and thyme, and bring to a simmer. Return the shallots to the pan. Simmer until the wine has reduced to three-quarters its original volume. Turn off the heat.

3. Heat the chile oil in a large frying pan over medium-high heat and fry the shrimp until they change color, 2–3 minutes on each side. Sprinkle with the parsley.

4. Remove the slices of chorizo from the red wine sauce and thread onto small skewers, alternating each one with a cooked prawn. Drizzle the skewers with the red wine sauce from the pan. Serve hot.

CLAMS in white wine, butter & herb sauce

2 pounds (1 kg) clams, in shell
1 cup (250 ml) dry white wine
3 tablespoons butter
2 cloves garlic, finely chopped
2 red chiles, seeded and thinly sliced
1 tablespoon chopped fresh chives
1 tablespoon finely chopped fresh parsley
1 tablespoon cornstarch (cornflour), mixed to a paste with 1 tablespoon cold water
  Freshly baked bread, to serve

Serves 6-8 • Preparation 20 minutes + 1 hour to soak • Cooking 10–15 minutes • Difficulty 1

1. Soak the clams in a large bowl of cold water for one hour.

2. Heat a large frying pan over high heat. Add the wine and bring to a boil. Add the clams, cover, and steam, shaking the pan occasionally, until the clams open. Transfer to a bowl. Strain the cooking liquid through a fine-mesh sieve into another bowl and set aside.

3. Wipe out the frying pan and add the butter, garlic, and chiles. Cook over medium–high heat for 2–3 minutes. Add the chives and parsley and sauté for a few seconds more.

4. Add the juices from the clams and return to a simmer. Add the cornstarch mixture, stirring until the sauce thickens. Mix the clams into sauce. Serve hot, with the bread.

MUSSELS with tomato sauce

Serves 4–6 • Preparation 30 minutes + 1 hour to soak
Cooking 25–30 minutes • Difficulty 2

2¹/₂	pounds (1.2 kg) mussels, in shell	1	(14-ounce/400-g) can tomatoes, with juice
3	tablespoons (45 ml) extra-virgin olive oil	¹/₄	cup (60 g) tomato paste
	Salt	¹/₃	cup (90 ml) water
4	cloves garlic, finely chopped	2	tablespoons finely chopped fresh oregano
1	onion, chopped		Salt and freshly ground black pepper
¹/₃	cup (90 ml) dry white wine		

1. Soak the mussels in cold water for 1 hour.

2. Heat the oil in a large saucepan over medium heat and sauté the garlic and the onion until softened, 3–4 minutes. Add the white wine and simmer for 2 minutes. Add the tomatoes, tomato paste, water, and oregano. Simmer for 10 minutes. Season with salt and pepper.

3. Add the mussels, cover, and simmer until they have opened, about 5 minutes. Discard any mussels that do not open. Serve hot.

SMELT fritters

Serves 4–6 • Preparation 10 minutes • Cooking 10 minutes • Difficulty 1

1	pound (500 g) smelts or whitebait	¹/₂	cup (75 g) all-purpose (plain) flour
2	shallots, finely sliced	2	large eggs, lightly beaten
2	teaspoons finely chopped fresh dill		Salt and freshly ground black pepper
	Finely grated zest of 2 untreated lemons	4	cups (1 liter) olive oil, for frying
2	teaspoons freshly squeezed lemon juice		Lemon wedges, to serve

1. Mix the smelts, shallots, dill, lemon zest and juice, flour, and eggs in a large bowl until well combined. Season with salt and pepper.

2. Heat the oil in a large, deep frying pan or deep-fryer until very hot.

3. Drop tablespoons of the mixture into the pan and fry for 2–3 minutes until golden brown. Serve hot, with the lemon wedges.

BAKED scallops

Serves 4–6 • Preparation 15 minutes • Cooking 10 minutes • Difficulty 1

4	tablespoons (60 ml) extra-virgin olive oil	¹/₂	cup (75 g) fine dry bread crumbs
1	pound (500 g) sea scallops	1	tablespoon finely chopped fresh parsley
	Salt and freshly ground black pepper	1	teaspoon freshly squeezed lemon juice
4	slices prosciutto, cut into squares about the size of the scallops		

1. Preheat the oven to 450°F (230°C/gas 8).

2. Heat 1 tablespoon of oil in a large frying pan over high heat and sauté the scallops for 1 minute.

3. Put the scallops in small ramekins or scallop shells and season with salt and pepper. Cover with pieces of ham. Combine the bread crumbs, parsley, lemon juice, and remaining 3 tablespoons of oil in a small bowl. Sprinkle over the scallops.

4. Place the ramekins or shells on a baking sheet and bake until just tender, about 5 minutes. Serve hot.

PAN-FRIED squid

Serves 6–8 • Preparation 20 minutes • Cooking 20–25 minutes • Difficulty 2

1¹/₂	pounds (750 g) squid tubes	1	teaspoon freshly ground black pepper
²/₃	cup (100 g) fine semolina	1	cup (250 ml) olive oil, for frying
1	teaspoon salt	1	lemon, cut into wedges

1. Cut each squid tube open along one side. With a sharp knife score inside the skin diagonally in both directions. Cut the squid into rectangles measuring about 1 x 2 inches (2.5 x 5 cm).

2. Combine the semolina, salt, and pepper in a small bowl. Heat the oil in a large frying pan or wok over high heat. Dip the squid into the semolina mixture, turning to coat well.

3. Fry in small batches until lightly brown and crisp, 3–4 minutes each batch. Drain on paper towels. Serve hot with the lemon wedges.

BAKED CRAB tapas

1/3 cup (90 ml) extra-virgin olive oil
6 shallots, finely chopped
2 cloves garlic, finely chopped
1 long red chile, seeded and finely chopped
2 meaty tomatoes, peeled, halved, and chopped
1/4 cup (60 ml) dry sherry
1/3 cup (50 g) fine dry bread crumbs
1 tablespoon finely chopped fresh parsley
1 tablespoon finely chopped fresh chervil
1 tablespoon finely chopped fresh tarragon
1 pound (500 g) crabmeat
3 tablespoons butter, chopped

Serves 6 • Preparation 45 minutes • Cooking 30–35 minutes • Level 1

1. Heat the oil in a large saucepan over medium heat. Add the shallots, garlic, and chile, and sauté until the shallots have softened, 3–4 minutes. Add the tomatoes and sherry and simmer until reduced a little, 10–15 minutes. Season with salt and pepper and set aside.

2. Preheat the oven to 400°F (200°C/gas 6). Combine the bread crumbs, parsley, chervil, and tarragon in a small bowl. Combine the crabmeat and tomato mixture in another bowl, stirring to combine, then divide among six small ovenproof dishes. Top with an even layer of bread crumb mixture and dot with the butter.

3. Bake for 15 minutes, until golden brown. Serve hot.

FRIED TUNA empanadas

1 recipe empanadas pastry (see page 26)

1 small red onion, finely chopped

1 (6-ounce/180-g) can tuna, drained

1 large egg, hard-boiled and chopped

1 tablespoon finely chopped fresh parsley

1 ripe tomato, peeled, seeded, and chopped

6 green olives, pitted and chopped

1 tablespoon extra-virgin olive oil

$\frac{1}{2}$ teaspoon hot paprika

Salt and freshly ground black pepper

4 cups (1 liter) olive oil, for frying

Serves 6 • Preparation 20 minutes + 2 hours to chill the pastry
Cooking 15–20 minutes • Difficulty 3

1. Combine the onion, tuna, egg, parsley, tomato, olives, olive oil and paprika in a bowl. Season with salt and pepper.

2. Roll out the dough on a lightly floured work surface to about $\frac{1}{4}$ inch (5 mm) thick. Cut out six 4-inch (10-cm) circles. Place 1–2 tablespoons of filling on one-half of each circle, leaving a border free of filling around the edges. Spread the beaten egg around the borders and fold the pastry over the filling. Use a fork to press down on the edges to seal .

3. Heat the frying oil in a large frying pan over medium heat to very hot. Fry the empanadas in two batches until golden brown, 6–8 minutes. Drain on paper towels and serve hot.

These delicious fritters are best served straight from the pan. Prepare the batter and shrimp ahead of time and cook just before serving.

SHRIMP fritters

1	pound (500 g) small shrimp, peeled
2	cups (300 g) garbanzo bean (chickpea) flour
1	tablespoon finely chopped fresh parsley
3	scallions (spring onions), white part and a little of the green tops, finely chopped
$^1/_2$	teaspoon sweet paprika
$^1/_2$	teaspoon salt + extra, to serve
1	cup (250 ml) olive oil, for frying
	Slices or wedges of lemon, to serve

Serves 4-8 • Preparation: 20 minutes + 1 hour to chill • Cooking 10-15 minutes • Difficulty 1

1. Put the shrimp in a medium saucepan. Cover with water and bring to a boil. Simmer until pink, 2-3 minutes. Drain, reserving $1^1/_4$ cups (300 ml) of the cooking water. Dry the shrimp on a clean kitchen towel. Chill until ready to cook.

2. Combine the flour, parsley, scallions, paprika, and salt in a bowl. Add enough of the cooking water to obtain a batter about as thick as pancake batter. Cover and chill for 1 hour.

3. Finely chop the shrimp with a knife. Stir into the batter.

4. Heat the oil in a large frying pan to very hot. Add tablespoons of batter and fry, turning once, until golden and crisp, 1-2 minutes each sides. Scoop out with a slotted spoon and drain on paper towels.

5. Sprinkle with a little extra salt, if liked, and serve hot with the slices or wedges of lemon.

If you liked this recipe, you will love these as well.

SMELT fritters

FRIED TUNA
empanadas

SALT COD FRITTERS
with allioli

CRISP CALAMARI with spicy red sauce

4 cups (1 liter) olive oil, for deep-frying

1 cup (150 g) all-purpose (plain) flour

1 pound (500 g) squid, cleaned and sliced into rings or scored

Salt

1 lemon, cut into wedges, to serve

1 recipe spicy red sauce (see page 34)

Serves 4–6 • Preparation 20 minutes + time for the spicy sauce
Cooking 10–15 minutes • Difficulty 2

1. Heat the oil in a deep fryer or deep saucepan to 375°F (190°C). If you don't have a frying thermometer, test the oil temperature by dropping in a small piece of bread. If it turns gold and bubbles to the surfaces the oil is ready.

2. Put the flour in a large bowl. Add about one-third of the calamari to the flour, toss gently to coat, then shake off the excess. Carefully add to the oil and deep-fry until crisp and golden, 3–5 minutes per batch. Remove with a slotted spoon and drain on paper towels.

3. When all the calamari are cooked, dust with salt, drizzle with the lemon juice, and serve hot with the spicy sauce.

FRIED anchovies

12   ounces (350 g) anchovies, cleaned
2   cups (500 ml) milk
$^1/_2$ cup (75 g) all-purpose (plain) flour
1   cup (250 ml) olive oil, for frying
    Salt

Serves 4 • Preparation 15 minutes + 30 minutes to soak • Cooking 10 minutes • Difficulty 1

1. Soak the anchovies in the milk in a medium bowl for 30 minutes. Drain well.

2. Put the flour in a large bowl. Add the anchovies, tossing gently, then shake off the excess.

3. Heat the oil in a large frying pan to very hot. Fry the anchovies in two batches until crisp and golden brown, about 5 minutes each batch.

4. Season with salt and serve hot.

This dish combines two classic Spanish flavors, salt cod and allioli (garlic mayonnaise). You will need to begin the day before as the salt cod must be soaked for at least 24 hours to rehydrate it. Change the water during soaking several times to remove the strong salty brine.

Allioli is a classic sauce from Mediterranean Spain. It is closely related to the classic provençal sauce of similar name, *aioli*. Traditionally served with meats, fish, and potatoes, it is very good on vegetables and bread too. There are many variations on the classic recipe.

SALT COD FRITTERS with allioli

Fritters

1	pound (500 g) salt cod
1$^1/_4$	pounds (600 g) floury potatoes, peeled
1$^1/_4$	cups (300 ml) milk
6	scallions (spring onions), finely chopped
2	tablespoons extra-virgin olive oil
2	tablespoons finely chopped fresh parsley
	Freshly squeezed juice of $^1/_2$ lemon
	Freshly ground black pepper
2	large eggs, lightly beaten
	Plain (all-purpose) flour, for dusting
1	cup (150 g) fine, dry bread crumbs
2	cups (500 ml) olive oil, for frying
	Lemon wedges, to serve

Allioli

2	large cloves garlic, finely chopped
$^1/_4$	teaspoon salt
2	large egg yolks
1$^1/_4$	cups (300 ml) extra-virgin olive oil
	Freshly squeezed juice of $^1/_2$ lemon

Serves 6–8 • Preparation 30 minutes + 24 hours to soak + 1–2 hours to chill • Cooking 15–20 minutes • Difficulty 3

Fritters

1. Soak the salt cod in cold water for 24 hours, changing the water two or three times. Drain well.

2. Cook the potatoes in a pan of lightly salted boiling water until tender, 15–20 minutes. Drain and mash until smooth.

3. Bring the milk and half the scallions to a simmer in a large saucepan. Add the soaked cod and poach until it flakes easily, 10–15 minutes. Remove the cod and flake it with a fork into a bowl, discarding the bones and skin.

4. Add 1 cup of mashed potato to the cod and beat with a wooden spoon. Work in the oil and gradually add the remaining potato, scallions, and the parsley. Season with lemon juice and pepper. Add half the egg and beat until thoroughly combined. Chill until firm, 1–2 hours.

5. Shape the chilled mixture into 16 small round cakes. Dredge in the flour, then dip in the remaining beaten egg, and coat with bread crumbs. Chill until ready to fry.

Allioli

1. Pound the garlic and salt in a mortar and pestle. Gradually whisk in the egg yolks. Beat in half the oil in a steady trickle. Beat in 1 tablespoon of lemon juice followed by the remaining oil until very thick. Add more lemon juice if liked.

2. Heat the frying oil in a large frying pan over medium-high heat. Fry the fritters until golden, 4–5 minutes. Turn and fry until golden on the other side, 4–5 minutes. Drain on paper towels. Serve hot with the allioli and lemon wedges.

meaty tapas

JAMÓN SERRANO croquettes

2   tablespoons extra-virgin olive oil
$^1/_4$ cup (60 g) butter
$^1/_3$ cup (50 g) all-purpose (plain) flour
$1^1/_2$ cups (375 ml) hot milk
$3^1/_2$ ounces (100 g) jamón serrano or prosciutto, finely chopped
     Salt and freshly ground black pepper
2   large eggs, lightly beaten
1   cup (150 g) fine dry bread crumbs
4   cups (1 liter) olive oil, for deep-frying

Serves 6–8 • Preparation 20 minutes + 4-12 hours to chill • Cooking 15-20 minutes • Difficulty 2

1. Heat the oil and butter in a saucepan over medium heat. Add the flour and cook and stir for 1 minute. Remove from the heat and stir in the milk. Return to the heat and cook, stirring constantly, until thickened, about 5 minutes.

2. Stir in the jamón serrano and season with salt and pepper. Cook for 1 more minute, then pour into a bowl and let cool. Chill until set, at least 4 hours or overnight.

3. Put the eggs in one small bowl and the bread crumbs in another. Shape the ham mixture into small croquettes. Roll in the bread crumbs, shaking off any excess, and dip in the beaten egg. Roll again in the bread crumbs, coating evenly. Lay in a single layer on a platter. Chill for 30 minutes.

4. Heat the frying oil in a deep-fryer or deep saucepan to very hot. Fry the croquettes in small batches until golden brown, 3-4 minutes each batch. Scoop out with a slotted spoon and drain on paper towels. Serve hot.

If you liked this recipe, you will love these as well.

BREAD FRITTERS
with salsa

HAM & SESAME
puffs

POTATO & HAM
croquettes

You will need tasty, ripe tomatoes for this dish. It is not always easy to tell in the supermarket which tomatoes will taste best and which will be bland. One way to check is to sniff them; if they have a lovely pungent tomatoey-smell, buy them. If they have no odor, leave them on the shelf.

ROASTED TOMATO & SERRANO toasts

Toasts

12	small-to-medium firm vine-ripened tomatoes, halved
24	cherry tomatoes
2	tablespoons extra-virgin olive oil
	Salt
12	thick slices firm-textured bread
3–4	cloves garlic, peeled
6	large slices jamón serrano ham, halved
1/2	cup (50 g) green olives, pitted and halved
2	tablespoons fresh parsley, to garnish

Sherry Vinaigrette

1/4	cup (60 ml) extra-virgin olive oil
1	tablespoon sherry vinegar
	Salt and freshly ground black pepper

Serves 6–12 • Preparation 20 minutes • Cooking 20–25 minutes Difficulty 1

Toasts

1. Preheat the oven to 400°F (200°C/gas 6). Arrange the tomatoes on a large baking sheet, halved ones cut-side up, Drizzle with the oil and season lightly with salt. Roast until softened, 15–20 minutes.

2. Spread the bread out on another large baking sheet and bake until crisp and golden brown, 4–5 minutes. Rub each slice with the garlic.

Sherry Vinaigrette

1. Whisk the oil, vinegar, salt, and pepper in a small bowl.

2. Top each slice of toast with the roasted tomatoes, ham, olives, and parsley. Drizzle with some vinaigrette and serve warm.

If you liked this recipe, you will love these as well.

TOMATO & ANCHOVY
bread

AVOCADO & HAM
toasts

HAM & CHEESE
bocadillos

AVOCADO & HAM toasts

1	baguette (French loaf), sliced
$\frac{1}{2}$	cup (120 ml) allioli (see page 82)
2	avocadoes, peeled, pitted, and sliced
4	large slices smoked ham, cut into pieces large enough to top the bread

Serves 6-8 • Preparation 15 minutes • Cooking 4-5 minutes • Difficulty 1

1. Preheat the oven to 400°F (200°C/gas 6). Spread the bread out on a baking sheet. Bake for 4-5 minutes, until crisp and golden brown.

2. Spread each slice with some of the allioli and top with a slice of avocado and smoked ham. Serve warm.

HAM & CHEESE bocadillos

4   bread rolls, halved
2–3   cloves garlic, peeled
2   ripe tomatoes, peeled and coarsely chopped
2   tablespoons extra-virgin olive oil
1   tablespoon sherry vinegar
      Salt and freshly ground black pepper
8   slices serrano ham
5   ounces (150 g) Manchego cheese, sliced

Serves 8 • Preparation 15 minutes • Cooking 4–5 minutes • Difficulty 1

1. Preheat the oven to 400°F (200°C/gas 6). Spread the bread rolls out on a baking sheet. Bake for 4–5 minutes, until crisp and golden brown.

2. Rub each bread roll half with garlic. Combine the tomatoes in a bowl with the oil, vinegar, salt, and pepper.

3. Spoon the tomato mixture over the bread rolls then top with the ham and cheese. Serve warm.

SALAMI with fresh figs

Serves 4–6 • Preparation 10 minutes • Difficulty 1

12	ounces (350 g) fresh green or black figs	
5	ounces (150 g) thinly sliced salami, rinds removed	

1. Arrange the figs and salami on a serving dish. If fresh fig leaves are available, place a layer on the serving dish before adding the figs and salami.

FIGS wrapped in ham

Serves 6 • Preparation 10 minutes • Cooking 20–30 minutes • Difficulty 1

12	ripe figs
12	slices jamón serrano
12	bay leaves

1. Preheat the oven to 325°F (170°C/gas 3).

2. Wrap each fig in a slice of ham and secure with toothpicks onto which a bay leaf has been threaded. Arrange the figs in a nonstick baking dish.

3. Bake until the figs are pink and a thick liquid has formed, 20–30 minutes.

4. Transfer to serving dishes and spoon the cooking juices over the top. Serve warm.

HAM & ASPARAGUS spears

Serves 4 • Preparation 15 minutes • Cooking 3–4 minutes Difficulty 1

20	asparagus spears, tough woody ends removed		Salt and freshly ground black pepper
	Freshly squeezed juice of 1 lemon	6	large slices prosciutto, cut in half
1/3	cup (90 ml) extra-virgin olive oil		Shavings of aged Manchego or Parmesan cheese

1. Blanch the asparagus in a large saucepan of boiling water until tender, 3–4 minutes, depending on the thickness of the spears. Drain and rinse in ice-cold water to stop the cooking process. Drain well.

2. Place the lemon juice in a small bowl. Slowly add the oil, whisking constantly, until the dressing thickens. Season with salt and pepper.

3. Wrap a slice of prosciutto around each asparagus spear and arrange on a serving dish. Pour the dressing over the top and sprinkle with the cheese shavings. Serve at once.

HAM & ASPARAGUS rolls

Serves 4–6 • Preparation 15 minutes • Cooking 10–12 minutes • Difficulty 2

2	tablespoons freshly grated Manchego or Parmesan cheese	6	sheets filo (phyllo) pastry
2	teaspoons finely grated untreated lemon zest	1/4	cup (60 ml) extra-virgin olive oil
1	teaspoon freshly ground black pepper	12	slices jamón serrano
1	teaspoon sweet paprika + extra, to dust	12	asparagus spears, tough ends removed
			Balsamic vinegar, to serve

1. Preheat the oven to 425°F (220°C/gas 7). Line a baking sheet with parchment paper. Mix the cheese, lemon zest, pepper, and paprika in a small bowl.

2. Lay out a sheet of filo pastry on a work surface. Fold in half lengthwise. Lightly brush with oil. Sprinkle with one-sixth of the cheese mixture. Cut in half lengthwise. Wrap a slice of ham around an asparagus spear. Place a pastry strip around the spear, winding in a spiral from the bottom. Arrange on the prepared baking sheet. Repeat with remaining ingredients to make 12 spirals. Dust lightly with paprika.

3. Bake until golden, 10–12 minutes. Serve warm with balsamic vinegar for dipping.

Sherry is widely used in Spanish cooking. This fortified wine is made from white grapes originally grown near Jerez de la Frontera, in Spain. It derives its English name from the anglicization of Jerez.

CHICKEN LIVER & SHERRY salad

Sauce
1/2   cup (25 g) fresh parsley
2   cloves garlic, peeled
4   tablespoons blanched hazelnuts
2   teaspoons hot smoked paprika
1/4   cup (60 ml) extra-virgin olive oil

Salad
3   ounces (100 g) blanched hazelnuts
2   tablespoons extra-virgin olive oil
1   tablespoon butter
1   pound (500 g) chicken livers, cut into bite-size pieces
1/2   cup (120 ml) dry sherry
2   tablespoons freshly squeezed lemon juice
   Salt and freshly ground black pepper
2   cups (100 g) arugula (rocket)
2   tablespoons sherry vinegar

Serves 4–6 • Preparation 10 minutes • Cooking 15 minutes • Difficulty 2

Sauce

1. Combine the parsley, garlic, hazelnuts, paprika, and oil in a food processor and pulse to a coarse paste.

Salad

1. Preheat the oven to 400°F (200°C/gas 6). Spread the hazelnuts on a baking sheet and roast for 5 minutes. Chop coarsely and set aside.

2. Heat the oil and butter in a large frying pan over medium-high heat. Sauté the livers until browned, 2–3 minutes. Add the sherry, and simmer until it evaporates. Stir in the sauce and lemon juice, and season with salt and pepper.

3. Toss the arugula with the vinegar and divide among four to six small serving plates. Spoon the chicken liver mixture on top. Sprinkle with the toasted chopped hazelnuts and serve warm.

If you liked this recipe, you will love these as well.

FAVA BEAN salad

FAVA BEANS catalan style

CALVES' LIVER with sherry

FAVA BEAN salad

1½   pounds (750 g) fresh fava (broad) beans

½   cup (120 ml) extra-virgin olive oil

¼   cup (60 ml) sherry wine vinegar

1   teaspoon tarragon mustard

  Salt and freshly ground black pepper

4   tablespoons finely chopped fresh mint

1   small onion, finely chopped

1   large tomato, cut into cubes

2   hard-boiled eggs, quartered

5   slices jamón serrano, coarsely chopped

  Freshly baked bread, to serve

Serves 6–8 • Preparation 15 minutes • Cooking 5–10 minutes
Difficulty 1

1. Cook the fava beans in a large pot of salted, boiling water until tender, 5–10 minutes. Drain well.

2. Whisk the oil, vinegar, and mustard in a small bowl. Season with salt and pepper.

3. Toss the fava beans, mint, onion, and tomato in a large salad bowl. Drizzle with the dressing and toss well.

4. Top with the eggs and jamón serrano. Serve with the bread.

FAVA BEANS catalan style

2 tablespoons extra-virgin olive oil

3½ ounces (100 g) bacon, diced

3½ ounces (100 g) blood sausage, sliced into rounds

1 medium onion, finely chopped

3 cloves garlic, finely chopped

2 large tomatoes, coarsely chopped

2 tablespoons finely chopped fresh mint

½ teaspoon cayenne pepper

1 cup (250 ml) dry white wine

4 pounds (2 kg) fresh fava (broad) beans, hulled

Salt

1 teaspoon sugar

Serves 8–12 • Preparation 15 minutes • Cooking 20–25 minutes
Difficulty 1

1. Heat the oil in a large frying pan over medium heat. Sauté the bacon, sausage, onion, garlic, tomatoes, mint cayenne pepper, and wine for 10 minutes.

2. Add the fava beans and season with salt and sugar. Cover and simmer until the fava beans are tender, 10–15 minutes. Serve hot.

This is a hearty tortilla that will make tapas for six to eight people or a main course for four. Be careful when putting the frying pan in the oven to broil (grill) as the handle may burn. To stop this from happening, wrap the handle in aluminum foil.

SPICY CHORIZO tortilla

5	tablespoons (75 ml) extra-virgin olive oil
8	ounces (250 g) spicy chorizo, thinly sliced
1½	pounds (750 g) waxy potatoes, thinly sliced
2	onions, thinly sliced
4	large eggs
2	tablespoons finely chopped fresh parsley + extra to garnish
1	cup (120 g) freshly grated Manchego cheese
	Salt and freshly ground black pepper

Serves 6–8 • Preparation 15 minutes • Cooking 50–55 minutes
Difficulty 2

1. Heat 1 tablespoon of oil in a large, deep frying pan over medium heat. Add the chorizo and sauté until golden brown, 4–5 minutes. Drain on paper towels.

2. Add 2 more tablespoons of oil to the pan and sauté the potatoes and onions for 2–3 minutes. Cover tightly and simmer over low heat, turning occasionally, until softened and slightly golden, about 30 minutes. Add a little water to the pan if the potatoes begin to stick.

3. Beat the eggs, parsley, cheese, chorizo, salt, and pepper in a large bowl. Gently stir in the potatoes and onions, taking care not to break up the potato too much.

4. Wipe the pan with paper towels and heat the remaining 2 tablespoons of oil. Add the potato mixture and cook over very low heat until the egg begins to set, 5–10 minutes.

5. Preheat the broiler (grill) to high. Place the tortilla underneath and broil until it is set and golden. Serve warm.

If you liked this recipe, you will love these as well.

TORTILLA
with arugula

CHEESE & HAM
toasts

HAM & MANCHEGO
tortilla

The sweetness of the dates melds beautifully with the salty flavors of the ham and cheese in these tasty little *pinchos* from northern Spain.

HAM-WRAPPED DATES with cheese

16   dates

16   pieces firm goat cheese

16   strips jamón serrano ham (or pancetta or streaky bacon)

1   cup (250 ml) olive oil, for frying

Serves 4–8 • Preparation 15 minutes + 1 hour to chill • Cooking 10–15 minutes • Difficulty 2

1. Cut a date open lengthwise, remove the pit (stone), and stuff with a piece of goat cheese. Roll a strip of ham around the stuffed date and fix in place with a toothpick. Repeat with all the dates, cheese, and ham.

2. Put the date and ham wraps on a plate and chill in the refrigerator for 1 hour.

3. Take out of the refrigerator about 10 minutes before frying.

4. Heat the oil in a large frying pan to very hot. Add half the wrapped dates and fry, turning carefully, until the cheese is melting. Drain on paper towels while you cook the others. Serve hot.

If you liked this recipe, you will love these as well.

SALAMI
with fresh figs

HAM & ASPARAGUS
spears

FIGS
wrapped in ham

SPICY CHICKEN & GARLIC skewers

1	pound (500 g) boneless chicken thighs, cut into chunks
4	cloves garlic, finely chopped
1	teaspoon hot paprika
1	tablespoon finely chopped fresh thyme
	Freshly squeezed juice of 1 lemon
3	tablespoons extra-virgin olive oil
½	teaspoon salt
½	teaspoon freshly ground black pepper

Serves 4–6 • Preparation 15 minutes + 1 hour to marinate • Cooking 10–15 minutes • Difficulty 1

1. Put the chicken in a bowl with the garlic, paprika, thyme, lemon juice, oil, salt, and pepper. Toss to coat well. Cover with plastic wrap (cling film) and marinate in the refrigerator for at least 1 hour.

2. Preheat a barbecue, grill pan, or overhead broiler (grill) to medium–high heat. Thread the chicken onto small skewers. Cook, turning and basting with the marinade, until the chicken is tender, 10–15 minutes. Serve hot.

GARLIC & CUMIN chicken wings

12   chicken wings

4   cloves garlic, finely chopped

     Finely grated zest and juice of 1 unwaxed lemon

1   teaspoon cumin seeds

1/3   cup (90 ml) extra-virgin olive oil

1/2   teaspoon salt

1/2   teaspoon freshly ground black pepper

3   tablespoons (45 ml) honey

Serves 6-8 • Preparation 15 minutes + 12 hours to marinate • Cooking 45–50 minutes • Difficulty 1

1. Use a sharp knife or kitchen scissors to cut the chicken wings at the knuckle to make 24 pieces.

2. Combine the garlic, lemon zest and juice, cumin, oil, salt, and pepper in a bowl with the chicken wings and toss to coat. Cover and chill in the refrigerator overnight.

3. Preheat the oven to 400°F (200°C/gas 6). Bake the chicken wings for 45–50 minutes until crisp. Drizzle with the honey 10 minutes before they are ready. Serve hot.

The Spanish word "migas" can be translated into English as crumbs. Migas are a traditional dish in the cuisines of southeastern Spain, made using yesterday's leftover bread. There are many variations on the basic recipe; this one comes from Almería, in Andalusia.

MIGAS de almería

102

2   pounds (1 kg) day-old, firmed textured bread

$1/3$ cup (90 ml) water

$1/3$ cup (90 ml) extra-virgin olive oil

8   ounces (250 g) bacon, diced

4   ounces (120 g) salami, diced

2   cloves garlic, finely chopped

1   teaspoon cayenne pepper

Serves 8–10 • Preparation 15 minutes + 12 hours to stand • Cooking 15–20 minutes • Difficulty 1

1. Crumble the bread into a large bowl. Drizzle with the water and let stand for 12 hours.

2. Heat the oil in a large frying pan over medium heat. Sauté the bacon and salami until well browned, 5–7 minutes. Transfer to a plate and set aside.

3. Sauté the garlic in the same frying pan until softened, 3–4 minutes. Season with the cayenne pepper and add the bread crumb mixture. Cook for 2–3 minutes then add the bacon and salami and cook for 5 minutes more. Serve hot.

If you liked this recipe, you will love these as well.

BREAD, ANCHOVY & CAPERBERRY salad

BAKED CRAB tapas

HAM & CHEESE bocadillos

BBQ MINI pork ribs

1½   pounds (750 g) pork ribs
¼   (30 g) all-purpose (plain) flour
½   cup (120 ml) sweet sherry
½   teaspoon Tabasco sauce
1   tablespoon tomato paste (concentrate)
1   teaspoon soy sauce
1   tablespoon brown sugar
   Coarse sea salt

Serves 6–8 • Preparation 15 minutes • Cooking 15–20 minutes
Difficulty 1

1. Preheat a barbecue or indoor grill to medium-high.

2. Separate the ribs and cut them into half across their width. Place in a large plastic bag with the flour and shake well.

3. Combine the sherry, Tabasco, tomato paste, soy sauce, and brown sugar in a bowl. Dip the ribs in the sauce and grill, turn occasionally, until charred and cooked through, 15–20 minutes. Sprinkle with salt and serve hot.

BBQ MINI pork kebabs

⅓ cup (90 ml) extra-virgin olive oil

1 teaspoon ground cumin

½ teaspoon thyme

½ teaspoon sweet smoked paprika

1 teaspoon red pepper flakes

1 bay leaf, crumbled

1 tablespoon finely chopped fresh parsley

Salt and freshly ground black pepper

1 pound (500 g) lean pork, cut into 1-inch (2.5-cm) cubes

Serves 6-8 • Preparation 15 minutes + 4-12 hours to marinate • Cooking 15-20 minutes • Difficulty 1

1. Combine the oil, cumin, thyme, paprika, red pepper flakes, bay leaf, parsley, salt, and pepper in a large bowl. Add the pork and stir to coat. Cover and refrigerate 4 hours or overnight, stirring occasionally.

2. Preheat a barbecue or indoor grill to medium-high. Thread the meat onto small wooden or metallic skewers.

3. Grill, basting with the marinade, until well browned but still juicy, 15-20 minutes. Serve hot.

Artichokes are native to North Africa and are widely grown and eaten in Spain. If you are not used to artichokes, the important thing to remember is to remove all the tough outer leaves. This may feel wasteful, but you really can only eat the very tender inner hearts.

ARTICHOKES with ham

3	pounds (1.5 kg) small, young globe artichokes
1	lemon, halved
2	tablespoons lard (optional)
1/3	cup (90 ml) extra-virgin olive oil
5	ounces (150 g) jamón serrano ham, diced
1	tablespoon finely chopped fresh parsley
	Salt

Serves 8–12 • Preparation 25 minutes • Cooking 30–40 minutes • Difficulty 2

1. Clean the artichokes by trimming the stalk and cutting off the top third of the bulb. Remove the tough outer leaves by bending them down and snapping them off at the base. When the tender heart is exposed, cut in half and remove any fuzzy choke with a knife. Rub the artichokes with the lemon half. Bring a large pan of salted water to a boil. Add the artichokes and simmer until tender, 20–25 minutes.

2. Drain the artichokes well, turning them upside down and pressing gently.

3. Melt the lard, if using, with the oil in a large frying pan over medium-low heat. Add the ham and artichokes and cook gently, stirring occasionally, for 8–10 minutes. Sprinkle with the parsley, season with salt, and serve hot.

If you liked this recipe, you will love these as well.

ARTICHOKE & MANCHEGO salad

FAVA BEAN salad

FAVA BEANS catalan style

PORK TENDERLOIN with whiskey

1	pork tenderloin, about 14 ounces (400 g)
	Salt and freshly ground black pepper
2	tablespoons extra-virgin olive oil
6	cloves garlic, finely chopped
2	tablespoons freshly squeezed lemon juice
$3/4$	cup (200 ml) whiskey
2	teaspoons cornstarch (cornflour)
$3/4$	cup (180 ml) beef stock
	Freshly baked bread, to serve

Serves 4 • Preparation 15 minutes • Cooking 10–15 minutes • Difficulty 1

1. Slice the pork tenderloin into fillets and season with salt and pepper. Heat the oil in a large frying pan over medium-high heat. Add the garlic and pork and cook the meat on both sides until browned and cooked through, 5–10 minutes. Set aside and keep warm.

2. Add the lemon juice to the pan, stirring rapidly on medium heat, then add the whiskey. Stir well, then add the cornstarch, whisking quickly to cook it slightly. Add the beef stock and simmer and stir until just thickened.

3. Return the pork to the pan and reheat. Serve hot with plenty of bread to soak up the sauce.

CALVES' LIVER with sherry

3   tablespoons (45 ml) extra-
    virgin olive oil
2   onions, chopped
1   teaspoon dried thyme
1   teaspoon dried basil
1   teaspoon dried parsley
    Salt and freshly ground black
    pepper
1   cup (250 ml) medium or
    sweet sherry
1   pound (500 g) calves' liver,
    cut into small cubes
4   thick slices crusty bread, cut
    into 1-inch (2.5-cm) cubes
1   tablespoon finely chopped
    fresh parsley

Serves 4–6 • Preparation 15 minutes • Cooking 15–20 minutes
Difficulty 1

1. Heat 1 tablespoon of oil in a large frying pan over medium-
    high heat. Add the onions and sauté until softened, 3–4
    minutes. Add the dried thyme, basil, and parsley, and
    season with salt and pepper. Add the sherry, decrease
    the heat to low, and simmer for 2–3 minutes.

2. Add the calves' liver to the frying pan and simmer until
    cooked through, 6–8 minutes.

3. Heat another small frying pan over medium-high heat.
    Drizzle the remaining 2 tablespoons of oil over the cubes of
    bread and add to the pan. Sauté until crisp and golden
    brown, 3–5 minutes.

4. Add the croutons to the pan with the liver. Garnish with the
    parsley and serve hot.

If you are preparing a spread of tapas, always include this one. It is a favorite with everyone!

110

MEATBALLS in tomato sauce

Serves 4 • Preparation 15 minutes • Cooking 15–25 minutes • Difficulty 1

8	ounces (250 g) ground (minced) beef
1	cup (60 g) fresh white bread crumbs
2	tablespoons freshly grated Manchego or Parmesan cheese
1	tablespoon tomato paste (concentrate)
3	cloves garlic, finely chopped
2	scallions (spring onions), finely chopped
2	teaspoons finely chopped fresh thyme
1/2	teaspoon turmeric
1	large egg, lightly beaten
	Salt and freshly ground black pepper
2	tablespoons extra-virgin olive oil
1	(14-ounce/400-g) can plum tomatoes, chopped, with juice
2	tablespoons dry red wine
1	tablespoon finely chopped fresh basil
2	teaspoons finely chopped fresh rosemary

1. Combine the beef, bread crumbs, cheese, tomato paste, garlic, scallions, thyme, turmeric, egg, salt, and pepper in a bowl. Shape the mixture into 12–15 small meatballs.

2. Heat the oil in a large frying pan over medium-high heat. Add the meatballs and sauté until browned all over, 5–7 minutes.

3. Add the tomatoes, wine, basil, and rosemary. Simmer gently until the meatballs are cooked and the sauce is reduced, 10–15 minutes. Season with salt and pepper and serve hot.

If you liked this recipe, you will love these as well.

MEATBALLS
with sage

CATALAN
meatballs

MEATBALLS
with almonds & peas

MEATBALLS with sage

Serves 6 • Preparation 15 minutes • Cooking 25–30 minutes • Difficulty 1

1½	pounds (750 g) lean ground (minced) beef	6	ounces (180 g) Manchego cheese, cut into small cubes
2	cups (120 g) fresh bread crumbs	¼	cup (30 g) all-purpose (plain) flour
¼	cup (60 ml) milk	¼	cup (60 g) butter
1	large egg, beaten	½	cup (120 ml) dry white wine
2	tablespoons finely chopped fresh parsley	1	sprig fresh sage
	Salt and freshly ground black pepper		

1. Combine the meat in a bowl with the bread crumbs, milk, egg, parsley, salt, and pepper and mix well.

2. Shape into meatballs the size of walnuts. Push a piece of cheese into the center of each one. Dredge the meatballs in the flour.

3. Melt the butter in a saucepan over medium heat. Add the meatballs and sage. Sauté until browned, about 5 minutes. Add the wine and simmer until it evaporates. Lower the heat, cover, and simmer until tender and cooked through, about 20 minutes.

4. Place on a serving dish and drizzle with the cooking juices. Garnish with the sprig of sage and serve hot.

MEATBALLS with grapes

Serves 4–6 • Preparation 20 minutes • Cooking 20 minutes • Difficulty 2

1	clove garlic		Salt and freshly ground black pepper
2	leaves sage	16	large seedless green grapes
2	sprigs rosemary		
1	pound (500 g) ground (minced) pork	⅔	cup (100 g) fine dry bread crumbs
½	teaspoon crushed fennel seeds	4	cups (1 liter) olive oil, for frying

1. Finely chop the garlic, sage, and the leaves of 1 sprig of rosemary. Mix the pork, chopped herbs, and fennel seeds in a large bowl. Season with salt and pepper. Carefully peel each grape. Shape the pork mixture into small balls the size of walnuts. Make a hollow in the center and press a grape inside. Close up the meatball.

2. Finely chop the remaining rosemary leaves and mix with the bread crumbs. Roll the meatballs in the mixture until well coated.

3. Heat the oil in a deep-fryer or large, deep frying pan to very hot. Fry the meatballs in batches until golden brown, 5–7 minutes per batch. Drain well on paper towels. Serve hot.

CATALAN meatballs

Serves 4–6 • Preparation 15 minutes • Cooking 5–10 minutes • Difficulty 1

1	pound (500 g) ground (minced) pork	⅓	cup (60 g) pine nuts
1	cup (60 g) fresh bread crumbs		Salt and freshly ground black pepper
2	large eggs, lightly beaten	½	teaspoon ground cinnamon
2	tablespoons finely chopped fresh parsley	½	teaspoon ground nutmeg
3	cloves garlic, finely chopped	½	cup (120 ml) olive oil, for frying

1. Put the pork in a large bowl and stir in the bread crumbs, eggs, parsley, garlic, pine nuts, salt, pepper, cinnamon, and nutmeg. Mix well.

2. Heat the oil in a large frying pan over medium-high heat and fry the meatballs until golden brown all over, 5–10 minutes.

3. Place the cooked meatballs on a preheated plate covered with paper towels to drain. Serve hot.

HAM & SESAME puffs

Serves 4–6 • Preparation 20 minutes + 4 hours to chill Cooking 20 minutes • Difficulty 2

½	cup (75 g) all-purpose (plain) flour	½	cup (60 g) diced ham
½	teaspoon baking powder		Salt and freshly ground black pepper
½	teaspoon sweet paprika	6	tablespoons sesame seeds, toasted
2	large eggs, beaten	4	cups (1 liter) olive oil, for frying
1	cup (120 g) freshly grated Manchego cheese		

1. Mix the flour, baking powder, and paprika in a bowl. Add the eggs, one at a time, mixing until just combined. Stir in the cheese and ham. Season with salt and pepper.

2. Shape the mixture into balls the size of small plums. Chill for at least 4 hours.

3. Roll the puffs in the sesame seeds. Heat the oil in a deep-fryer or large, deep frying pan to very hot.

4. Fry the puffs in batches until puffed and golden brown, 5–7 minutes per batch. Drain on paper towels and serve hot.

Meatballs are common tapas and are served in bars and restaurants all over Spain. In our recipe, the meatballs are dredged in almonds, which adds a delicious flavor to the sauce.

114

MEATBALLS with almonds & peas

8	ounces (250 g) ground (minced) veal
5	ounces (150 g) ground (minced) pork
$^1/_2$	cup (60 g) finely chopped bacon
1	onion, finely chopped
2	large eggs, lightly beaten
1	cup (60 g) fresh bread crumbs
	Salt and freshly ground black pepper
$^1/_2$	cup (75 g) finely ground almonds
$^1/_4$	cup (60 ml) extra-virgin olive oil
1	medium tomato, peeled and coarsely chopped
3	cups (750 ml) water
2	cups (300 g) peas

Serves 4–6 • Preparation 15 minutes • Cooking 30 minutes • Difficulty 1

1. Combine the veal, pork, bacon, half the onion, eggs, bread crumbs, salt, and pepper in a large bowl.

2. Put the almonds in another bowl. Add tablespoons of the meat mixture and shape into balls the size of walnuts.

3. Heat the oil in a large frying pan over medium heat. Sauté the remaining onion until lightly browned, 4–5 minutes. Add the tomato and simmer for 5 minutes.

4. Pour in the water and season with salt. Add the peas and meatballs. Cover and simmer over low heat until the meatballs are tender and cooked through, about 20 minutes. Serve hot.

If you liked this recipe, you will love these as well.

MEATBALLS
in tomato sauce

MEATBALLS
with sage

MEATBALLS
with grapes

POTATO & HAM croquettes

1   pound (500 g) potatoes, peeled
1   tablespoon butter
$1/2$ cup (120 ml) milk
2   large eggs, 1 separated
1   cup (150 g) all-purpose (plain) flour
$3^{1}/_{2}$ ounces (100 g) jamón serrano ham, finely chopped
     Salt and freshly ground black pepper
$1/2$ cup (120 ml) olive oil, to fry
$1/3$ cup (50 g) fine dry bread crumbs

Serves 4–6 • Preparation 25 minutes + 1 hour to chill • Cooking 30–40 minutes • Difficulty 2

1. Cook the potatoes in salted boiling water until tender, 20–25 minutes. Drain and mash with the butter until smooth. Gradually add the milk, 1 egg yolk, and the flour, mashing until stiff. Stir in the ham. Season with salt and pepper.

2. Take tablespoons of the mixture and shape into croquettes. Chill in the refrigerator for at least 1 hour to firm up.

3. Heat the oil in a large frying pan over medium heat. Whisk the remaining egg white and egg in a bowl. Put the bread crumbs in a bowl. Dip the croquettes in the egg and then roll in the bread crumbs.

4. Fry the croquettes in batches until golden brown, 3–5 minutes each batch. Scoop out with a slotted spoon and drain on paper towels. Serve hot.

CHEESE & HAM toasts

2 slices jamón serrano ham
4 slices white or brown toast bread, crusts removed
2 slices Manchego cheese
Freshly ground black pepper
3 large egg whites
1/3 cup (90 ml) milk
1/4 cup (60 ml) extra-virgin olive oil

Serves 4-8 • Preparation 20 minutes • Cooking 10-15 minutes
Difficulty 1

1. Place a slice of ham on two pieces of bread and cover with cheese. Season with pepper and top with the remaining bread, pressing down firmly so the slices stick together.

2. Whisk the egg whites and milk in a bowl. Cut the sandwiches into quarters and add to the bowl with the egg mixture. Turn after about 5 minutes so that they soak up all the egg mixture.

3. Heat the oil in a large frying pan over medium heat to very hot. Add the sandwich quarters and fry until golden brown, 3-4 minutes. Turn and fry on the other side until golden brown. Serve hot.

We have used a mixture of ham and chorizo to flavor this tortilla. but you could use one or the other.

HAM & MANCHEGO tortilla

4	tablespoons (60 ml) extra-virgin olive oil
3¹/₂	ounces (100 g) jamón serrano ham, finely chopped
2	ounces (60 g) chorizo, thinly sliced
1	small sweet red onion, thinly sliced
1	clove garlic, finely chopped
1	pound (500 g) potatoes, very thinly sliced
6	large eggs
	Finely grated zest of 1 unwaxed lemon
	Salt and freshly ground black pepper
2	ounces (60 g) Manchego, thinly shaved + extra to serve
¹/₃	cup coarsely chopped fresh parsley
1	recipe allioli (see page 82)

Serves 6–8 • Preparation 15 minutes • Cooking 20-30 minutes
Difficulty 1

1. Heat 2 tablespoons of oil in large ovenproof frying pan over medium-high heat. Add the ham and chorizo and sauté until crisp, 2–3 minutes. Transfer to a plate with a slotted spoon and keep warm.

2. Return the pan to the heat and add the remaining 2 tablespoons of oil. Add the onion and garlic and sauté until softened, 3–4 minutes. Add the potatoes and sauté until tender, 4–5 minutes. Set aside.

3. Whisk the eggs and lemon zest in a bowl. Season with salt and pepper and pour over the potato mixture. Gently stir in the Manchego, parsley, and ham mixture.

4. Preheat an overhead broiler (grill) to high. Place the frying pan over medium heat and cook, shaking the pan frequently, until set on the bottom, 6–8 minutes. Broil the top until golden and set, 4–5 minutes. Serve warm with the allioli.

If you liked this recipe, you will love these as well.

TORTILLA
with arugula

SPICY CHORIZO
tortilla

CHEESE & HAM
toasts

INDEX